Faith and Manifestations

Overcoming Warfare Within the Mind

By
ALANA STARR MOORE

Copyright © 2024 by ALANA STARR MOORE

Faith and Manifestations

Overcoming Warfare Within the Mind

All rights reserved. This book or any portion of it may not be reproduced or used in any manner whatsoever without the author's express written permission except for the use of brief quotations in a book review. Printed in the United States of America

Published by: Royal Kingdom Publishing
www.keyottacollins.com

Royal Kingdom
PUBLISHING

Scripture quotations are from King James Version of the Bible and New International Version of the Bible

"Discovering our pathway to manifestations, towards what God has already said about our life and future."

-ALANA STARR MOORE

Jeremiah 29:11 KJV

"For I know the thoughts that I think toward you, saith the Lord, thoughts of peace, and not of evil, to give you an expected end."

Dedication

To all those who are affected by mental health challenges, warfare in the mind, life situations, and self-development. This book is dedicated to you.

In sharing a part of my life, may you discover in this book that God makes no mistakes. Everything you've ever gone through has a purpose because He cares for you. I pray that you realize that faith is an action word you use daily in every area of your life.

I'm so thankful for the opportunity to serve you and I pray that you gain from this book what's needed in your life and that it will give you the power and encouragement to know that God is always able to deliver us all, according to your faith.

1 John 4:4 KJV

Ye are of God, Little children, and have overcome them: because greater is He that is in you, than he that is in the world.

Table of Contents

Introduction 1

Chapter 1: Life Obstacles, The Manifestation of a Trigger .. 3

Chapter 2: Denial and The Rejections 10

Chapter 3: The Danger of The Wrong Coping Mechanisms 17

Chapter 4: Warfare In the Mind and How to Overcome ... 23

Chapter 5: The Reality of Challenges 32

Chapter 6: Acceptance Towards a Better You and Tomorrow 38

Chapter 7: Faith That Moves Mountains Life and Death Is in the power of Your Tongue 44

Chapter 8: Encourage Yourself 51

Chapter 9: Positive Patterns Equals Better Habits 58

Chapter 10: A New Lifestyle 63

Chapter 11: The Knowing and Realization of You Are Never Alone 72

Chapter 12: It's a New Day and a New You 79

Chapter 13: Life With Peace 85

Chapter 14: Wellness and Balance in The Mind 90

Chapter 15: Look How far You've Come You are A Successor Because of Your Progression 98

Chapter 16: Maintenance and Up-Keep The Qualities of Life 104

    Alana's Proclamation 112

    Acknowledgments 114

    A Message from My Family to You 117

    An Invitation to Salvation 124

    The Response 125

References 126

To my Lord and Savior Jesus Christ,

Thank you for who you are and all that you truly mean to me. Thank you for being the author and finisher of my faith. I know that your love is unfailing and unmatchable. For that alone, I strive to honor you with my life and express my gratitude towards you in every detailed way, even as I interact with people from all over the world, from different walks of life, regardless of who they are or what they choose to believe. I shall demonstrate love in all I do because you are love.

With All My Heart Your Daughter,

Alana

Letter to the reader

Greetings to you! I want to introduce myself formally. My name is Alana Starr Moore, and I am a woman of Great Faith. I want to thank you for taking the time out to read a part of my life, that I pray will help bring clarity to yours. It is my desire for you, as you read this book to be enlightened, empowered, encouraged, and motivated as you continue to journey through life with hope, recognizing that it's your faith in the God within you that can shift your life continuously, as you may grow. I love you and most importantly, God loves you more, yes you!

Humbly Summited,

Your Sister in Christ Alana

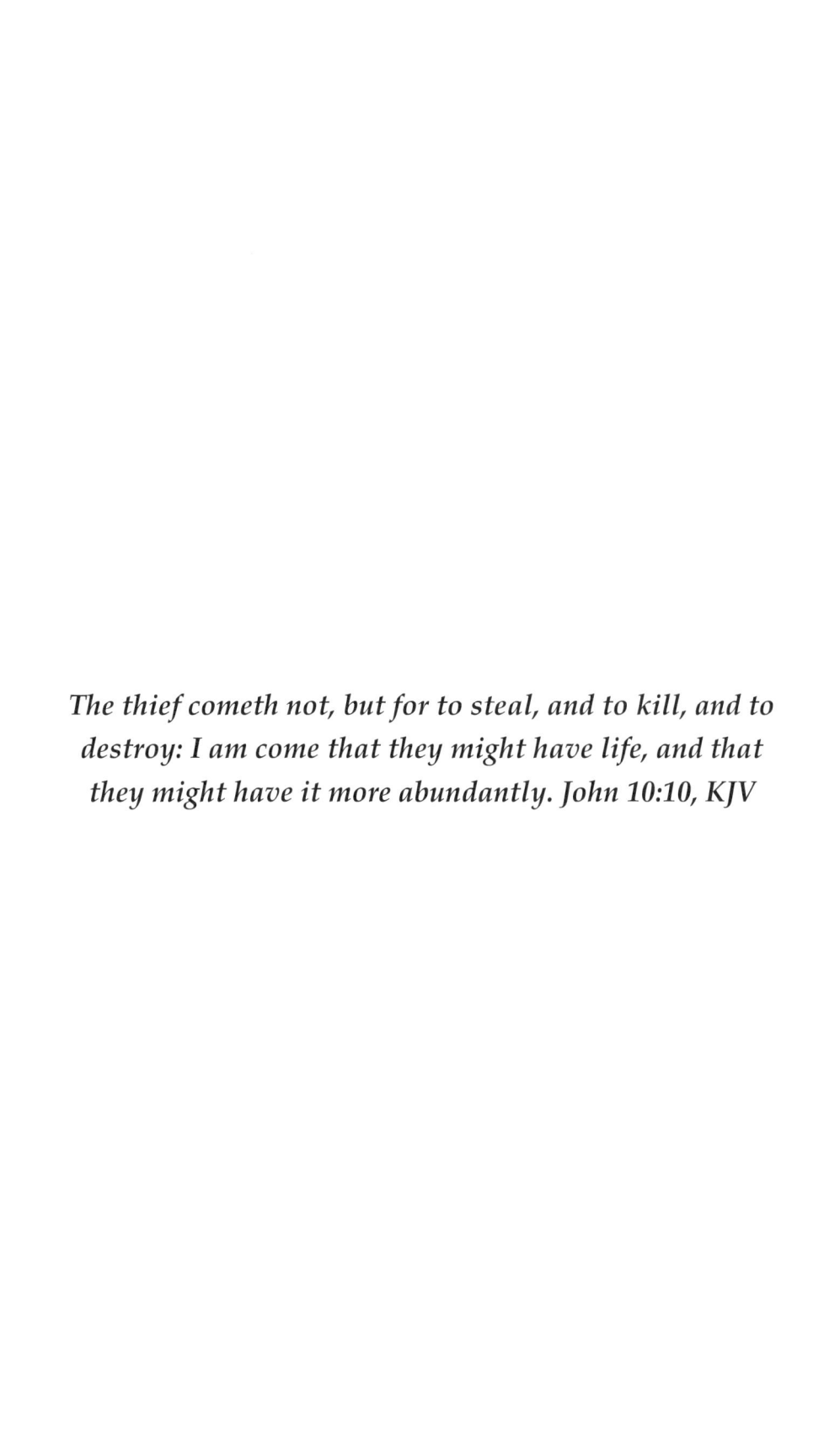

The thief cometh not, but for to steal, and to kill, and to destroy: I am come that they might have life, and that they might have it more abundantly. John 10:10, KJV

INTRODUCTION

Hello! How are you feeling today? Are you happy, sad, have anxiety, or maybe even depressed? If you have felt, and or happen to feel either one, it's ok if you do. How so? For starters, we all have those moments in life, no matter where we are on our journey. I'm not saying that it's ok to be sad or to fester in anything that would prohibit you from entering in a positive direction, but from a personal standpoint; I do understand. When you know what type of feelings and emotions you have, regarding your state of mind, you are aware. Believe me when I tell you, I have experienced them all and many others. Say this with me, "I am not alone."

Do you have moments in life where you're happy because everything around you and all of whom is connected to you are on the upside of things? If you can relate, let's go deeper. Have you ever had a moment where you were saddened by an event that took place in your life, and you became suppressed by it? Is it possible that maybe you felt like your situation seemed hopeless and things just got worse, which caused a built-up frustration that turned into depression? If you can relate, let's go deeper. Can we? Have you ever experienced happiness and sadness at the same time? You have? Wow! And you are still here, reading these words! Mm…mmm! I'm not sure If you know this or have been told, but you are an overcomer and more than a conqueror. Just like me!

I welcome you to join me as I share a part of my life and how I gained insight into how to live a stable and balanced lifestyle. I am a woman whose faith is in God and who has suffered from bipolar and insomnia. Truth is, I still do but it is well managed because of my willingness to endure to the end. If I didn't have my savior Jesus Christ on my side, I would have never survived any of those vicious battles.

Mental health is on the rise in today's world. There were times when I wanted to give up on life because I was overwhelmed by the massive warfare in my brain. My psychiatrist provider stated, "It's like a twenty-four-seven war," whenever you are in a manic state and having an episode. I know this to be so true and real.

I want you to gain from this book hope, faith, determination, and knowing that you must be willing to still fight for your well-being, even when it seems like it's no use. The Bible says, *And he said unto me, My grace is sufficient for thee: for my strength is made perfect in weakness. 2 Corinthians 12:9 KJV.* Know that the good Lord is there by your side even though a lot of times you can't see Him nor feel Him, He is present and is always available to you. Coming up in church, I would hear the elders say… "He may not come when you want Him to, but He's always on time." Beloved, I want you to hang in there and hold on because I just believe that your breakthrough is coming! I connect my faith to yours.

CHAPTER 1

Life Obstacles, The Manifestation of a Trigger

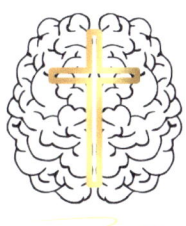

Hello, sunshine! I'm unsure if you are aware of it or not, but deep within you there is a light. And if you feel like your switch is off, can I tell you that I've been there, too? God has said to us all, *Let your light shine before men, that they may see your good works, and glorify your Father which is in heaven. Matthew 5:16 KJV.* So, don't dim your light but instead, let it shine bright. May I share with you how a particular trigger altered my life? And how I was able to flip the switch on again, and in return learned how to keep it on.

Having light makes our path a lot clearer. When there is no light, we have no good sense of direction. The uncertainty of the "unknown" can potentially create a trigger that can become disastrous. I welcome you to join in with me as I visit a time in my life when I had my first episode (of many) that stemmed from a trigger and the outcome of it wasn't so great.

It was year 2006, located in Durham NC. I was eighteen years old. During this period of my life, I got married and endured a lot of stress from the relationship. Also, I had people in my life that didn't mean me any good. All I knew was that I wanted to be loved (so I thought). I came to realize that I was loved. I had a loving family. Growing up my parents was and still is an amazing representation of a healthy marriage within the household, thank God. Therefore, it is what I desired for myself. Before this life-changing event occurred, I had never experienced this type of stress before, ever. Something came over me that changed my entire state of mind and mood. Stress.

I remember one day I stayed home from school because I didn't feel right, my thought pattern was off. During this time, I was under the impression that my grandmother was about to pass away and was having visions of her walking on clouds. I felt a strong water connection as well. I felt as though God was using it as a tool to speak to me. I felt so different than I had ever felt, I was in total discomfort. So, I ended up going to my high school because I didn't want to be alone. When I arrived at the school I went into the front office and talked to the front office lady. I shared with her what this voice was telling me about myself and my grandmother. I was very paranoid because I was under a strong impression that my grandmother was about to die.

After I was done expressing myself to her, she responded to me and said, "God is with you," and that I didn't need to be afraid. After that, I ended up leaving my high school and headed home. By this time my mental state had escalated to another level. My mom ended up coming home from work to check in on me and pretty much discovered me in a manic state. She went on to ask me questions and to her discovery, as I began to answer them, she quickly realized that I needed medical attention, immediately. I then confessed to her that I was not exactly sure as to what was happening to me but "Please Mommy take me to the doctor," I said. So, we got in the car and headed over to Duke Hospital for psychiatric help. I must say, I was never violent, nor did I want to hurt myself or others, not ever. It was the voices in my brain that at that time took me for a loop because it was completely out of the norm for me.

Once I got to Duke Hospital and was all checked in, from there I was then placed in the psychiatric ward. It was but so much that they could do for me so my mom had me transferred to a mental health facility. I remember during that process as I was being transferred, I rode in the back of a police car. It made me feel sad like I had done something wrong. It was nighttime, raining and storming outside that evening. When I arrived at the facility, they did my intake. I remember them placing me in this room that looked like a regular office-like setting. I sat down calmly in the seat that was before me and suddenly, within a blinking of an eye the lights went completely out, leaving me in total darkness because there were no windows.

As soon as the lights went out, I shouted out, "Jesus, Jesus, Jesus" (as I was raised to do so). I was crying out to Him. Because all I could think of was that He was with me like the front office lady told me. Honestly, that moment was me facing my fears. Because back then I was afraid of the dark. After a few minutes or so, the lights eventually came back on. And boy was I relieved. Shortly after, I was checked in fully and then escorted to a room that I was assigned to.

Honestly, to this day I know even more that God was personally reassuring me that He was with me in whatever state I was in. Whether my light is on and I'm shining bright or when it's low and I'm in a darkened state. When the afflictions of life and obstacles occur, He is more than able to deliver us all. It doesn't negate His presence from our lives but often makes Him show up even greater. *And we know that all things work together for good to them that love God, to them who are called according to His purpose. Romans 8:28, KJV.* The enemy has a way of how he uses his devices against us but no matter what we must believe and trust in our deliverer, the one who can do all things but fail in any given situation.

Know that you are never alone, even when those darkest moments occur, He's nearest the most. Before you can see the light, you must feel it first. Meaning that it's that inner feeling within our spirit (the mind) that lets you know that whatever you are seeking or needing, shall happen regardless of how it may seem. You may be in a state of mind where it's difficult for you to even try to feel hopeful. I recall a scripture that my mother taught me when I was a child when I asked her "Mommy what is faith?" she then told me *Now faith is the substance of things hoped for, the evidence of things not seen, found in the book of Hebrews11:1 KJV.* Just because it hasn't happened yet or God may not seem to be there, does not mean that it won't come to pass. You have got to already see it before it even happens, that is how you have faith and be in faith, you must put it to work within your thoughts, and once you are in faith, this is when it becomes active and activated within you. Your faith must be bigger than what you fear. This is how you defeat the enemy and win against the warfare within the mind.

Chapter 1 Reflection

Life Obstacles

The Manifestation of a Trigger

Now faith is the substance of things hoped for, the evidence of things not seen. Hebrews11:1, KJV.

And we know that all things work together for good to them that love God, to them who are called according to His purpose. Romans 8:28, KJV.

Self-Reflection:

What are your triggers?

_____
_____
_____
_____
_____

What obstacles do you need to overcome?

_____
_____
_____
_____
_____

What are your fears?

_____
_____
_____
_____
_____

CHAPTER 2

Denial and The Rejections

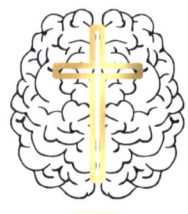

From what I have discovered when we are not honest with ourselves about our issues, we tend to put them off because of shame, guilt, or maybe even disappointment and the list goes on. Either way, we neglect them because we don't want to feel rejected by others. I can tell you sunshine, I've been there too. I was once in denial about this mental health challenge that I have dealt with. For one thing, back then I felt like I didn't want to be associated with anything that would label me as "crazy." Because of the stigma that is connected to the word's mental health. So, I decided to do something about it by starting with me. I started my quest and began to obtain a better understanding of my life, and those who can relate to me.

As a black woman, I understand the massive effect of the stigmatic presence that is happening within my culture and how so many of us are suffering in silence because of the lack of understanding and fear, as well as others all around the world. It is my desire for those of you who are bound by this preconceived notion or know of anyone who is to be completely free, in your mind, body, soul, and spirit. Everyone on the face of this earth, whether rich or poor, is in good health or not. We all have issues that are challenges that we face often that are different one from another, however, we still have them. The flip side of this is learning how to live and cope with them as you endure because the secret is you having control over them all and not it over you. Know that you are not what you are dealing with or have dealt with. You are stronger than you realize.

For starters, according to Bing, the definition of *Stigma* is a mark of disgrace associated with a particular, circumstance, quality, or person. According to the *American Psychiatric Association*, over half of people who have a mental challenge do not receive the help that's needed. People generally avoid it or put off seeking treatment because of concerns about being treated differently or losing their jobs. APA researchers have identified the different types of stigmas. You have *Public Stigma*- which is the negative discriminatory attitudes that others have about mental challenges*. Self-Stigma*- is the negative attitudes towards yourself, and personal shame about your challenge. *Institutional Stigma*- is systemic and involves government and private organizations that intentionally or unintentionally limit opportunities for those with a mental challenge. Often, lower funding for research, fewer mental health services, and health care are the outcomes.

According to the *American Psychiatric Association*, the *stereotypes* and *prejudice* about mental challenges are as follows: With **Public Stigma** people are viewed as dangerous, incompetent, to blame for their challenge, and unpredictable. As a result of this, the discriminatory effect is lower employment turnover ratings, rejection for housing, and low health care standards. *Self-stigma* is when individuals feel as though they are the blame, incompetent, and dangerous within. These thoughts lead to low self-esteem and the lack of confidence to have control over one's own motivation and social environment. This is where most people begin to develop the misperception that you are unworthy of good health. **Institutional Stigma** has law-binding stipulations within the government and institutions that place limits on opportunities and privileges. The more you know, the more you will grow. Educating yourself is the first step towards breaking the stigmatized influence that is impressed upon you.

I remember when the word came out that I was on the psychiatric word, again. I was so embarrassed for people to even know it. Check this out, I eventually heard through the grapevine that I was "crazy." Now, why did I have to hear that? I was a young lady who didn't have much experience or knowledge of mental health other than my first episode. All I knew or had knowledge of during that time was that it meant that you were crazy, and I refused to accept that association. This very thing caused me to deny the fact that I have a mental health challenge.

After hearing that I was called crazy, I completely began to live my life in a way that had no connection to my previous battle. I was determined that I would just forget it as if it had never happened. It was then that I fell into denial.

I felt rejected and abnormal because during that time I wasn't completely aware that stress was a major trigger for me. And that it caused me to become unbalanced if it wasn't released properly. So, I just continued my life from there on without any consciousness as to what happened to me. Listen, get this…because I decided to deny this challenge I have, not only did I suffer from rejection and judgment from others, but most importantly, I ended up rejecting myself and my overall well-being without realizing it. By not addressing this issue, such as educating myself, getting an understanding of this condition, and how to live with it, it just seemed much easier to forget about it all around. So, I never talked about it, ever. Nor did I admit to myself or anyone else that I struggled with this challenge. And my life during that time reflected it. I had to face the ridicule of people looking down on me, the loss of friendships, and persecution from people who knew nothing about what I was struggling with, the battles I faced, and how they affected me and impacted my life. This journey was a tough road to travel because I quickly learned that I needed to prioritize myself, my life, and ultimately my health. I had to be there for myself just like how I was always there for those who were connected to me during that time. When I needed them the most, they were no longer present in my life. I got to a place where I was not as ashamed and soon realized that all the pain I suffered, ridicule, judgment, and shame was not just for myself but for those who are afraid of being heard because of discrimination and not freely able to use their voice.

So, sunshine my advice to you is to never reject yourself, your thoughts, and your feelings because they will arise for many types of reasons, but ultimately it will teach you a lesson in return. Now, I'm not saying that everything you feel is true or right but it's always worth getting an understanding so that you can differentiate what is fact and what is not. Get this….in doing so you learn and discover things about yourself that you never knew, that might just enlighten you about who you are. So please don't ever be in denial about yourself, or issues or sweep them under the rug like I did because it only creates bigger problems for yourself, with no resolution. And always remember that the worst rejection is self-denial.

Chapter 2 Reflection
Denial and The Rejections

The righteous cry, and the LORD heareth, And delivereth them out of all their troubles. The Lord is nigh unto them that are of a broken heart; And saveth such as be of a contrite spirit. Psalm 34:17 & 18, KJV.

Self-Reflection:

Who are you?

_____
_____
_____
_____
_____
_____

What are your dreams and purpose?

_____
_____
_____
_____
_____
_____
_____

What changes do you need to make to position you to fulfill your purpose in life?

_____
_____
_____
_____
_____
_____
_____
_____
_____
_____
_____

CHAPTER 3

The Danger of The Wrong Coping Mechanisms

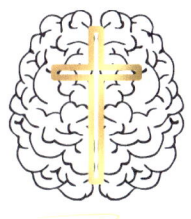

I get it sunshine! We all have our ways as to how we deal with our problems, stress, anxiety, issues, heartache, hurt, and much more. What I have discovered, personally, is that whatever issue there may be within your life, the overall determining factor is how you choose to go through those storms. If we choose to allow ourselves to change our perception of the situation we are going through, it makes the ride a lot smoother. Such as saying to yourself, let me sit back and assess this matter. I have this and that going on over here, but it's but so much that I can do. For example, you say to yourself let me just breathe, take a walk, pray to clear my thoughts, and come back to the issue. This gives you the advantage and opportunity to address the matter with a leveled and balanced thought process (within the mind), that in return will help you choose a better and more conducive method and or strategy for yourself and others, as you cope with the many issues of life.

Listen, I know all too well that it's much easier said than done. It's easy to say, "This too shall pass" and "It's going to be all right," until you must live it out as you're journeying through life. I know that feeling. I had gotten to a place where I was introduced to marijuana and began smoking. It became a mask for me. It took me to a place of temporary escape until I came back down and sobered up to find out that my issues were still there. I didn't realize the causes and effects it had on my mind. I was just settling for a short-term getaway and relief. I had no idea that I was coping with an unresolved mental health challenge during that time. And the mechanism I was utilizing was marijuana. Some people that I recalled could smoke it and be completely functional (so they thought, to an extent). As for me, it was different. I had to be completely done with everything for the day and then have a joint. Why? Because once I became intoxicated or "high" if you will, I would get paranoid.

During these moments I just seem not to function normally. All along, not realizing that I was causing the levels of dopamine and serotonin in my mind to produce abnormally. Before I break this down to you. I'll be the first to say that I'm not a practicing M.D. So, please seek medical professionals for your healthcare needs. I researched why I would feel "off" during those intoxicated times, and to my discovery, according to *Medical News Today*, I learned that neurotransmitters are part of the nervous system and are chemical messengers in the body. Their function is to transmit signals from one nerve cell to target cells and according to *Bing's* research Dopamine is a type of neurotransmitter in the brain that acts as a chemical messenger that transmits signals within our body. It is often referred to as a feel-good chemical and plays a crucial role in mental health. It is also associated with how we feel emotionally, it connects sensations of pleasure to specific actions, and how we behave, and react.

According to Bing's research, in conjunction with this, Serotonin is another type of neurotransmitter that regulates your mood within the mind. When Serotonin levels are normal, you tend to feel more focused, emotionally stable, happier, and calmer. On the other hand, low levels of serotonin are associated with conditions like depression. Also, according to Bing's research Serotonin together with Dopamine plays a role in our quality of sleep, how well we sleep, the sleeping time, and how long we can stay asleep. Serotonin makes melatonin, which is a hormone that regulates your sleep-wake cycle. According to *Sleep Doctor,* the sleep-wake cycle determines a person's level of sleepiness or wakefulness throughout the day and night. This further explains why I felt "off," I was chemically unbalanced within my mind by the marijuana because it counteracted against the abnormalities, I was already facing with me having a mental health challenge, psychologically.

Because I engaged in this activity, it blindsided me from every angle. My skin started to react with eczema (all over my body) and the tone of my lip color changed. It started to affect me negatively. What I discovered from those experiences is that when we have challenges in life, we don't take the time to properly assess them, to know and have a better understanding of how to discern the right strategy for a solution, instead, we continue a dead-end pathway that only makes the situation more massive than it initially was. And that is what happened to me.

There are a few scriptures that I'd like to share that talk about being content either when you are up or down regardless of whatever state you may be in. Your current situation or past doesn't have the power to dictate over you unless you allow it, but can permit the ability to withstand it successfully, through the mist of it all. Let's go there together, can we? *Philippians 4:11-13 KJV says, Not that I speak in respect of want: for I have learned, in whatsoever state I am, therewith to be content. I know both how to be abased, and I know how to abound: everywhere and in all things I am instructed both to be full and to be hungry, both to abound and suffer need. I can do all things through Christ which strengtheneth me.*

Beloved, I want you to know that this is how we should posture our minds, so that they may project the appropriate behavior, feelings, and emotions, while we are dealing with the many different types of adversities within our lives, whether personally or what's happening around us. Know that you can get through it because the good Lord is your strength. Stop trying to fight it alone because you will always feel defeated. Seek out the appropriate help even if you must reach out to others, don't be ashamed because this could be a pivotal turning point in your life, have faith, and trust that God will lead you to the right person and or people, and He will do the rest. Don't continue living in a repeated cycle of bondage and turmoil that is masked with things that are not beneficial to your life, health, and well-being. Don't get involved with people and things that will devalue who you are, but instead, relinquish those things unto God and allow Him to fill those voids. If what you've been trying to do is not working and being unsuccessful time, after, time, after time. This means that change is needed, in the right direction. Give up those wrong coping mechanisms and allow God to give you new solutions with much better outcomes. The right change is just waiting to happen for you!

Chapter 3 Reflection

The Danger of The Wrong Coping Mechanisms

Not that I speak in respect of want: for I have learned, in whatsoever state I am, therewith to be content. I know both how to abased, and I know how to abound: everywhere and in all things I am instructed both to be full and to be hungry, both to abound and suffer a need. I can do all things through Christ which strengthens me. Philippians 4:11-13, KJV.

Self-Reflection:

What mechanisms can you implement to help solve your issues?

_____
_____
_____
_____
_____
_____
_____
_____
_____
_____
_____
_____
_____
_____
_____

CHAPTER 4

Warfare In the Mind and How to Overcome

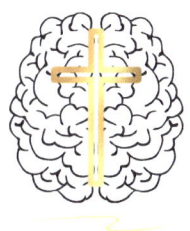

Wow! Sunshine, I know you or someone close to you have experienced warfare in your mind, especially today. I'm sure we all can attest to this, indeed. It may be or have been a mental crisis for you, anxiety, stress triggers, sadness, depression, low self-esteem, and the list goes on. Our minds are powerful because they reflect who we are in every aspect of our lives. The operation of our minds demonstrates our emotions, thoughts, and feelings. How you choose to think changes the dynamics of how you process things, whether good or bad, and in return permits the outcome of our situations in life. Our thoughts will eventually become who we are. How? It's simple. Because the bible says be ye transformed by the renewing of the mind.

Now I'm not a practicing M.D., but I do have a broad amount of past life experiences, that I'm just sharing with you. Because ultimately, it is my desire for you to receive whatever it is that's needed in your life and for someone else, that will make an impactful difference. Beloved, this means that every day you are feeding your mind with what it needs all according to what's fitting for your lifestyle. Your spirit resides within the mind. This is why we must be careful who and what we allow to enter it. When dark moments occur, and you have succumbed to a constant routine of awareness as to how your thoughts generate, they in return give power to your words. You will find yourself realizing what the scripture says in *Proverbs 18:21 KJV Death and life are in the power of the tongue: And they that love it shall eat the fruit thereof.* Yes, it sounds simple, but very powerful, transforming, and could very well change the trajectory of your life.

I recall a time in my life when I was impacted by this mental health challenge that I have. At this time in my life, I was living in Jacksonville Florida. I was two weeks in without any sleep, whatsoever. When I would lie down at night it seemed like the warfare or battle, if you will, would just become more massive. It would intensify itself to the highest. Being a woman of faith who knows what God can do, and trying to stand firm on that while the enemy was trying to take total control over my mind, was extremely difficult. It would be random thoughts out of nowhere like "You are nothing," or "Where is your God now?" The enemy was trying his hardest to convince me that there was no need to fight against him because he would say to me "You belong to me," or so he thought. By the second week, I was completely sleep-deprived, so my mom ended up having to fly into Jacksonville Florida from Durham North Carolina. During this time, my eldest sister and I lived together. My state of mind was very anxious, and I wasn't eating much at all.

The different thoughts kept cycling in and out of my mind from the enemy, such as "You are about to die" and "Just give up." I was at war in my mind. It was a torturous battle that was preventing me from sleeping at night. So, I ended up getting my bible and found the scripture *Proverbs 3:4 KJV that says, and thy sleep shall be sweet.* Next, I placed it under my pillow (out of desperation). I was in search of any breakthrough of whatever I could make happen, to relieve myself so that I could sleep (sometimes you must get desperate enough for a miracle). Finally, I laid down and within seconds I went off to sleep for like an hour or so. That one hour seemed like five hours' worth of sleep. It powered me up, so much so, to the point where I told my mom to take me to get medical attention because I was ready to go. I knew that it meant being placed in the psychiatric ward and being enclosed, but I didn't care because I could no longer continue suffering. I was never violent or wanted to harm myself or others. It was an unbearable spiritual warfare all in my mind. All the while, I could feel God's presence with me, letting me know that He was there every step of the way.

Next, we left the house to seek help. When my mom and I got into my black Ford Mustang there was a leakage on the passenger side that I had for quite some time, especially when it rained. So, every time it rained it would leave a puddle on the floor. As soon as I opened the door to get in the passenger side, I instantly smelled the smell of vinegar, very strongly. Within that moment, my spirit thought of the scripture when Jesus said, "I thirst" and they gave him vinegar on a sponge to drink. I turned to my mom and said, "Mama, do you smell that?" "No, I don't, what is it?', she said. I then said, "It smells like vinegar in here." As I got ready to sit on the seat, the top of my big toe (I had on sandals) slightly touched the puddle of the water that had built up in my car (because it stormed the night before) and immediately, I withdrew my toe very quickly. I felt the quickening in my spirit to draw back how I did. Honestly, it felt like God himself consecrated that puddle of water on the passenger side of my car because when I made contact with it, I felt His power. So, from there, we left in search of help for my mental state.

The first place we went to they couldn't help me. I took it as though it wasn't the right appointed place God wanted me to go. So, we ended up going to a hospital called Baptist Health. When we arrived, I walked into the Emergency Room department. There was a lady at the desk. She asked me, "What brings you in tonight for your visit?" and I replied, "I haven't slept in two weeks, I'm completely sleep-deprived, and my thoughts are in disarray." From there I was checked in and shortly after escorted to a bed in the hall, with my mom. As I was waiting, a nurse came up to me and said, "What's going on honey?" I said to her, "I haven't slept in two whole weeks, zero sleep." She walked away and then came back. She said to me, "Well honey the doctor has ordered you some meds that will help you sleep, but it will be a shot because it works faster by going through your bloodstream quicker." I didn't want the shot, but I agreed with it. She left to go get the materials for the injection. When she came back, it was time for me to receive the shot. So, I turned my head and closed my eyes. As soon as the needle pierced my skin, immediately afterward my heavenly language came forth (for the first time) in a diverse tongues type of way, like it's stated in the Bible in *1 Corinthians 12:10 KJV*. Instantly, what came to my mind was when they pierced Jesus' side after He was already dead. I remember seeing multiple nurses' men and women from different cultural backgrounds greeting me, as the diverse tongues were manifesting. Each of them was very kind to me. After twenty minutes or so, I began to feel sleepy, the medication started to take effect.

    Shortly after, I was transferred to a room. I got out of the wheelchair and got up onto the bed. A nurse entered and said, "How are you feeling?" I replied by saying, "I feel the medication kicking in and my sleep coming forth." She then told me, "Well, honey we are going to transfer you to the psychiatric ward." And from there I told my mother, "I'll see you when I get out, I love you." From there I was willed to the ward. I remember when I arrived there, it was a white woman who came up to me as if she knew me and we began talking. She happened to have a blanket with blue and white colors on it and a purple kitten/lion (a stuffed animal). She went on to ask me, "Why are you here?" My reply was, "I can't sleep." Suddenly, she threw the blanket over my head and the divers tongues came forth again, but on a different level. God used that woman to catapult me into a dimension I had never experienced, in the realm of the spirit. It was a supernatural encounter with God in that place, on the psychiatric ward.

Directly after that, I began praying and warring within the spirit, but in tongues. I proceeded to walk down the hall and simply laid hands on the lady's door post and said a prayer, continued my way back down the hall, all while still in the spirit for hours (God was moving by his power on that psychiatric ward). After I came out of the spirit and was then in the natural. I started walking back up the hall and suddenly, I began to hear a loud snore. I mean it echoed throughout the entire ward. So much so that I went to the nurse station and asked, "Who is that snoring so loudly?" She said, "It's your friend, she's sleeping!" As if she was implying that she hadn't slept in a long while, herself. I believe it because the sound of that snoring told it all. And get this…I had the lady blanket over my head throughout that encounter with God. The blue and white blanket reminded me of a prayer Shaw. The purple kitten/lion (stuffed animal) made me think of God's royalty, with Jesus being the lion of Judah. These two items were symbolic of God being supreme authority. All of what she had in her procession, were tangible biblical messages, from God that he was about to set the atmosphere for His power to be revealed so that He can get the Glory.

Listen sunshine, if I didn't have Jesus on my side, I would have lost that war that was going on in my mind and deliverance would not have never taken place. Thank God there is no failure in Him. Because all I knew at that time was that God was with me. When our minds are attacked, it takes a complete toll on us, our lives, and how we function. In my turmoil, God still saw fit to use, messed up broken Alana and deliverance took place. Just like He did for me, he can and will do the same for you. I know you're wondering how I might be used if I feel unusable. The answer is simple, surrender. Stop trying to figure out everything on your own without having a sound mind for good decision-making, when you are overwhelmed with stress and life, trying to decide on which path to take the frustration alone can misguide you into further chaos. Instead, I recommend that you begin to cast all your issues upon Him like He has stated in the word of God for us all.

You may even be dealing with something right now that may seem unbearable. Do you know that God's word says that He won't allow you to be tempted beyond what you can bear but provide a way of escape so that you may be able to withstand it, *1 Corinthians 10:13 KJV*? Wow! How loving is that? Beyond words! So beloved, when life becomes too much to handle, just release it all totally unto Him, He that can do all things but fail, have faith, and watch Him move miraculously on your behalf. This may even be new to you and probably doesn't make any sense, but that is the mystery of faith, and when you trust that God will do that very thing in your life that's needed, even when it seems impossible and doesn't make any sense. This is how God can truly demonstrate who He is, in His divine power. He will take the foolish things to confine your thoughts because His ways and thoughts are much higher than ours, as the word of God says. I'm reminded of the scripture that says, *Many are the afflictions of the righteous: but the LORD delivereth him out of them all Psalm 34:19 KJV*. So be encouraged and as my Daddy likes to say, "hold fast to your faith", which means don't let it go, no matter what comes your way.

Chapter 4 Reflection

Warfare In the Mind and How to Overcome

Death and life are in the power of the tongue: and they that love it shall eat the fruit thereof. Proverbs 18:21, KJV.

Many are the afflictions of the righteous: but the LORD delivereth him out of them all Psalm 34:19, KJV.

Self-Reflection:

Do you believe that there is deliverance within your warfare?

_____
_____
_____
_____
_____
_____
_____
_____
_____
_____
_____
_____
_____
_____
_____
_____
_____

CHAPTER 5

The Reality of Challenges

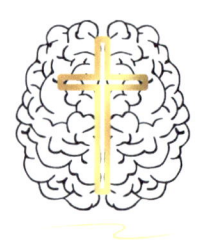

Listen sunshine, it's ok and even if it's not, it will be. We all have the challenges that we face. Some big. Some small. And as we journey through life, a lot of times it's difficult to prevent them from happening. In most cases, a challenge comes about for different reasons. It could be to strengthen a weak area in your life, another could be an unexpected event to take place, or maybe even a personal one you voluntarily placed yourself on and many others. Life has a way of surprising us with what I like to call, "pop-ups." Things and situations that just occur out of nowhere. From a personal standpoint, when I came to the realization that I have this mental challenge, and if not paired with the proper treatment, I would be challenged severely. From there, it became my reality.

To be honest; it was not something that I wanted to welcome into my life. But I knew that if I didn't accept this challenge, I would cause more harm than good. So, from there I decided that I would be intentional about how I choose to care for my mind and overall well-being. In doing so, I discovered that I needed to take medication (as a lifestyle change). By God's grace and mercy, I've never had to be on medication because I had a clean bill of health most of my life. I was the type of person who didn't like to take medication, so the initial acceptance of this ordeal was very hard for me. So, I faced it head-on without even trying to figure it out all at once. I started a type of medication during that time and stayed on it for a few years. It worked fine and I was able to take it while pregnant with my son, successfully. Years later I realized that I needed a different type of medication that worked for bipolar and insomnia. Eventually, I ended up working myself down to a lower dosage.

What I realized was that the medication assisted me with preventing the symptoms of having higher levels of dopamine in certain areas of my brain. Let me explain further. Upon my research according to Bing, I discovered that dopamine is a chemical that is released in the brain that makes you feel good. Now, having the right amount of dopamine is important both for your body and for your brain because it sends messages to your nervous system, that controls everything within the body. This is why the thoughts in your brain can seem so massive to you during those episode moments, from a scientific point of view.

Seemingly so, I'll be the first to say that I'm not a doctor, by far. However, I am someone who has suffered a great deal of warfare within the mind.

Beloved, I said all of that to say this, in life, we often keep ourselves from facing challenges because of fear, without understanding that it could be the various obstacles that can transform your life and make you stronger and more fit for the task ahead. From a personal point of view, I had to learn how to just go for it and face it, while keeping myself anchored in the Lord. And I encourage you to do the same thing too. Because the outcome of it just might be beyond your expectations. And know this, if you tried the first time and weren't as successful as you hoped. As I have said before there is no failure in God so try again.

You go ahead and approach that challenge in life in a joyful state of mind, even if you must force yourself. Because what you are doing is creating the right attitude and willpower that in return sets the right atmosphere (no matter where you are located) for you to be successful. So, face it, that very thing that you are fearful of, have faith and watch God work it out. Sometimes if not careful, fear can overrule the very thing that's meant to be a positive change within your situation that is presented right before your eyes. Your focus might be completely centered around that very thing, issue, or dilemma that blocks you from seeing the positivity in your reality. I understand how you can become consumed by it, and it may even appear to be a hopeless situation. Can I tell you that this is not true? It is a lie. This is a trap and attack from the enemy to keep you stuck and bound within your mind/spirit. This is a device that he uses to prohibit you from elevating your faith and dependency on God. If he can keep you from having any hope and takes away your joy you have allowed him to have the upper hand in your situation. If God is the same savior who made a way in the sea and a path in the mighty waters for a way of an exit, then He can surely do the same for you. In *Hebrews 13:8 KJV says, Jesus Christ the same yesterday, and today, and forever.* This means that He is the same God from the past, in the present and future. He doesn't operate in our time but within His divine timing which is the best timing. So, don't allow your challenges to control you. Take your power back and walk by faith because there is a lesson to be learned that will prepare you for that next level in life, but you must pass this test. Say to yourself, "I am not my challenge, but I am who God says that I am, and He will get me through this."

Chapter 5 Reflection

The Reality of Challenges

The thief cometh not, but for to steal, and to kill, and to destroy: I am come that they might have life, and that they might have it more abundantly. John 10:10, KJV.

My brethren, count it all joy when ye fall into divers temptations; knowing this, that the trying of your faith worketh patience. But let patience have her perfect work, that ye may be perfect and entire, wanting nothing. James 1:2-4, KJV.

I can do all things through Christ which strengtheneth me. Philippians 4:13, KJV.

Be careful for nothing; but in every thing by prayer and supplication with thanksgiving let your requests be made known unto God. Philippians 4:6, KJV.

Self-Reflection:

When facing challenges, what is necessary for you to succeed?

_____
_____
_____
_____
_____
_____
_____
_____

CHAPTER 6

Acceptance Towards a Better You and Tomorrow

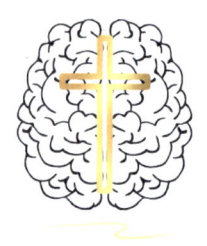

Your struggles, setbacks, heartaches, trials, tribulations, death of a loved one, and so on. These situations don't define you but make and shape you into the person that you are today. Sometimes we must accept our realities before we can overcome them. It's ok to say to yourself, I have this issue, but this issue doesn't have me. Because it can change. And it will change. But you must be willing to go through the process, first. This is where the real work begins towards a better you.

Sunshine, I know. I'll be the first to admit it. I wanted a change in my life and a better me overall. I kept saying it and thinking to myself, repeatedly, time after time. So, I concluded and realized that I had to accept the duration period that came along with it. It was by God's grace alone, that my eyes became open. It seemed like most of my peers and people my age appeared to be a lot further ahead in life and never seemed to deal with some of the battles that I faced. I got pregnant with my son Jacob, without being married, willingly, with me being who I am in Christ Jesus. At that time, I just assumed that his father and I would be together until the end. So, I thought.

After the relationship ended. The state of my reality from the breakup became an issue for me. Not to discredit Jacob's dad. It just didn't work out. Love will make you do things, won't it? I felt comfortable enough to allow myself to become impregnated because I believed that we were in it for the long hall such as marriage. So, because of this, I had to work even harder for a better me for the sake of my child, while still working towards a better future for the both of us.

Now let me explain, this was extreme for me because stress began to arise within my mental state. So, I had to fight every day, even harder just to uphold and maintain a balanced mindset as I grew into motherhood, as a single parent. I thank God for my parent's and family's support because, without their help in all the many times I needed them, I would not have successfully made it this far (I give honor to God for using them to be there for me).

Honestly, I just cannot stress this enough. What got me through back then and still is getting me through is my faith in God. I tried my hardest to stay close to Him in every area of my life in such an intricate way. And even when I made mistakes. Every week Jacob and I were in church, I sang in the choir and served in the community. I consistently listened to music that uplifted my spirit and said to myself, "My best is yet to come." I was very intentional about how I raised my son and still am. Even down to what he watches on TV and what type of music he listens to. To this very day.

I worked at Biltmore Elementary for Duval County Public School as an ESE paraprofessional teacher. I worked with students who all had different disabilities. I enjoyed the job because it taught me a lot about myself that I didn't know, such as patience (which I'm daily cultivating). One day one of my students said to me, "Ms. Moore, I'm coming home with you!" I laughed and smiled at him. I was so thankful because those precious babies were learning as I taught them and thriving academically. Little did they know they were helping me.

So, beloved I say unto you this day, go ahead and accept it, whatever it may be that seems like there is no hope. I'm a witness and living proof that it will change. Some may say how Alana? As I have said before, just be willing enough to go through the process. Listen, I had no idea that things were not going to work out with my son's father. And after going through the emotions and my feelings, I realized that being a mother to my son and learning how to do so, was far more important than the break-up itself. I had to forgive, let go, and move on. Because if I'd allowed myself to stay in a state of stress I was in because the relationship didn't work out, and worried about the three of us not being a "family," my priorities would've been out of order. Being a single mom has taught me and still is teaching me that I am a lot stronger than I thought. And that when I am tested the most is when I'm able to survive it, overcome it, and find myself succeeding beyond my expectations. How? All because of God's grace and mercy.

Trust me sunshine, you'll never know what you are capable of until you accept that very thing and not reject it. Because from there is where you begin the real work towards a better you. Self-improvement begins with you. And giving yourself permission to be processed, to let you see that in life, I may have issues to occur, but one thing is for sure. I will get through them all, and ultimately in the end, I shall win. This is the mindset that you should have and maintain as you are being processed for the necessary transitions in life. Every new day is a blessing and opportunity presented to you that gives you a choice to decide on how you should posture and position yourself to accept the things that you can change in your life, in the right direction and how you can work towards the things that may require more of you but in time, the desired transformation will happen, but you must be willing to do the work that's needed so that you can have a successful launching onto the right path. I understand how most of us want instant gratification, but it doesn't always happen in that sense. When you give yourself grace as you prepare for a better you and your future, you must have patience with yourself so that you can gain all the important things that are needed to help further prepare you for your new self. In doing so, you discover who you truly are, your strengths, weaknesses, and what your identity is. This is an act of faith that helps you to form and create a lifestyle that is full of endless possibilities that are manifestations of God's power and glory being revealed in your life.

When will the process begin for you? Don't put it off any further. Do what you can today and don't wait until tomorrow. I guarantee you that once you take the first step, you'll find yourself saying "That wasn't so bad", not realizing that the first step you took shifted your disposition in such a way that enabled your thought process to change, that can potentially encourage you to take the next step and so forth after that, and before you know it, you have succumbed to the right kind of change that's needed for your life and overall wellbeing. Welcome to a new chapter in your life and it's called acceptance.

Chapter 6 Reflection

Acceptance Towards a Better You and Tomorrow

Trust in the LORD with all thine heart; and lean not unto thine own understanding. In all thy ways acknowledge him, and he shall direct thy paths. Proverbs 3:5-6, KJV.

Self-Reflection:

What will you do to make a greater difference for your tomorrow?

_____
_____
_____
_____
_____
_____
_____
_____
_____
_____
_____
_____
_____
_____
_____
_____
_____
_____

CHAPTER 7

Faith That Moves Mountains
Life and Death Is in the power of Your Tongue

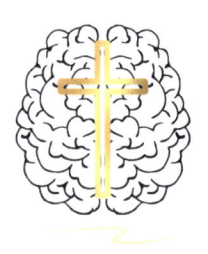

Beloved, I am a firm believer that your words have power. *Proverbs 18:21* says it here, *Death and life are in the power of the tongue: And they that love it shall eat the fruit thereof.* The words you speak are powerful and can change your mindset and bring forth manifestations according to what you say, positively or negatively. It is imperative to be mindful and aware of how you process things within the mind before you release them into the atmosphere.

In February 2023, I was dealing with some health insurance discrepancies, with them denying me approval for the medication I'd taken for five years consecutively, without any issues or episodes. I called my insurance company (at that time) the next day and they said to me, "Ma'am we have denied your claim because according to our bylaws, it appears to us that there is no medical need for this medication." I then said, "If I send you all my medical records, will this suffice?" She replied, "Yes ma'am, but you would have to wait and call us back within seven days for processing." I then began to explain that I could not go that long without the medication. So, I ended up going nine days without medication that had been helping me all the while.

Now, I could have asked my family to help me purchase the medication (out of pocket), but I didn't because it was very expensive. I didn't want them to worry about me. I felt as though it was my burden to carry and not theirs. So, I began to lose sleep each night, more and more, total restlessness. I would hear thoughts in my mind but honey, by this time, and given past experiences, thankfully so, God taught me how to differentiate when it was Him speaking, myself, the world, and the devil (now I don't endorse you to getting to this point, this level of understanding came from the many past episodes/experiences and encounters). I had gotten to a point where I mastered it. Get this... I tried so hard to not allow my son to see the symptoms within me throughout that entire ordeal.

I still had to carry on with my normal routine with my motherly duties, as if nothing was happening, such as homework, learning activities, playtime, dinner time, quality time, our time, and bedtime. Thankfully, he couldn't notice, and I was determined for him not to. Finally, on the ninth day, Jacob and I were home in Jacksonville Florida. And the doorbell rang, it was my parents. Now, get this. I had just prayed earlier that day to God and said, "Lord I can't go on like this any further, this is torture for me, please help me!" Sure enough, He did just that, and right on time to be exact. My parents could discern in the spirit that I was spiraling downward mentally. Shortly after their arrival, it was time to pick my son up from school. So, my parents and I left the house to pick him up and then headed back home.

From there I decided that I needed to go and get medical treatment. I was determined that my situation would be fixed and if it meant getting admitted into the psychiatric ward so be it, I knew within myself that it wouldn't be a long stay. I had to use my faith to get me through, as I was suffering, to maintain my levels of dopamine because, at this point, I was completely sleep-deprived. I went to the hospital and got admitted to the psychiatric ward and ended up staying for two-and-a-half days. During that short stay, I witnessed the miraculous take place right there in the hospital, on the ward. It was my second day there. It was nighttime after dinner and about an hour before they started to distribute the medications. There was an allotted time for patients to relax and settle themselves down before the night concluded. So, during this downtime, I decided that I wanted to separate myself from the other patients and sit somewhere quietly so that I could write. So, I grabbed my black-and-white composition notebook and started walking down the hall towards the eating area where there were tables and no people. As I walked past the phone area there was a woman who was sitting, and as soon as I got closer to her, she blurted out at me. I simply opened my mouth to respond, and my heavenly language came forth, and instantly her entire body started to shake drastically as she was sitting in the seat. I recognized that she had an unclean spirit operating within her and that deliverance was taking place.

I proceeded to head to my desired area and thought nothing of it afterward. I grabbed a seat and started to write in my notebook. When it came time for the medication distribution, I walked down to the nurse station and noticed that the same woman who blurted out at me was sitting in the recliner chair calmly reading what appeared to look like the Bible. I was amazed because I knew that the power of God that came forth from my mouth brought forth deliverance and she was set free. I was building myself up in spirit before I arrived at the hospital, long beforehand because I was in great warfare. I was constantly talking to God daily because I understood that He was the only way to help me endure what was happening to me. I was in deep warfare every day, but I was determined to stay connected to God and remain anchored in my faith.

I chose to speak life into what appeared to be a dead situation. Listen to this, in the book of *Mattew 17:20 KJV* it says, *And Jesus said unto them, Because of your unbelief: for verily I say unto you, If ye have faith as a grain of a mustard seed, ye shall say unto this mountain, Remove hence to yonder place; and it shall remove; and nothing shall be impossible unto you.* Isn't this so powerful to know that you can change the outcome of your situation by thinking about it first, then decreeing it out of your mouth, and paired with declaring the word of God over it? Wow! Beloved, know that you can speak to the mountain in your life, and yes, it shall move, but it's all according to your faith and the power of God that's within you. I'm not sure if you know this, but God has given you power within that He will allow you to unlock so that you can start learning how to use it against the warfare that rises before you. If you are unsure how to obtain this God-given power, start by praying and asking the Lord to teach you how and maybe even creating a situation that will activate the gifts and power of God that He has placed in you before the foundation of the earth. An act of faith and trust in the Lord almighty is what is required. This isn't much but how you choose to apply it depends on you.

Chapter 7 Reflection

Faith That Moves Mountains

Life and Death Is in the power of Your Tongue

Now unto Him that is able to do exceeding abundantly above all that we ask or think, according to the power that worketh in us. Ephesians 3:20, KJV.

Death and life are in the power of the tongue: And they that love it shall eat the fruit thereof. Proverbs 18:21, KJV.

And Jesus said unto them, Because of your unbelief: for verily I say unto you, if ye have faith as a grain of a mustard seed, ye shall say unto this mountain, Remove hence to yonder place: and it shall remove; and nothing shall be impossible unto you. Mattew 17:20, KJV.

Self-Reflection:

When you believe and have faith, what is hindering you?

_____
_____
_____
_____
_____
_____
_____
_____
_____

CHAPTER 8

Encourage Yourself

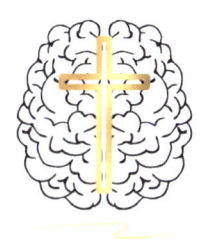

What about encouragement? Often, we may seek or desire encouragement from others and messages that address our situation because we all need to be encouraged at some point in our lives. Having someone there to offer support can be very uplifting. But what happens when they are not there to do so? What do you do? This is what I like to call a teaching moment because there is a message and a lesson to learn, to get you to that next point in life. And it starts with you. The ultimate and Supreme Authority who you should seek for any given assistance Is Jesus Christ. He has the power to give you exactly what is needed in your life and is the lifter of your spirit. The word of God is the Bible which is our life manual. Once you become saved and filled with God's spirit He gives you divine understanding, interpretation, and revelations according to His word and its relevancy to your life and others, when you pray and ask Him for it.

A few years ago, I was reflecting on my life during my time in elementary school. I'll be transparent and tell you that as a child, around the age of five and up, I loved to play like all children. I didn't value my academics as much as I should've, and it showed in my grades. I didn't have good studying habits, and, in my mind, I had no use for them. My mother did enforce academics within the household, but I just didn't want to comply (during that time).

By the third grade, I was placed on an IEP plan, which stands for Individualized Education Plan throughout grade school, middle school, and high school. It's a program in most schools designed to ensure that a child with an identified disability receives specialized instruction. This came with different types of services. For instance, when I would take a test, I would take it outside of the normal classroom setting, along with another teacher. When I was in the fourth grade, I remember taking the EOG (end-of-grade) testing. I recall myself just marking anything on my test because I just wanted to get it over with. When the results came back, I failed. And had to repeat the fourth grade over again. It didn't affect me until that moment. As I matured, I became ashamed of it and myself. Because I knew that I had a lot more to demonstrate academically than what I'd been displaying, all along.

During my senior year in high school, in my English 4 class, we had an assignment to write a paper. I didn't put much effort into the paper as I don't remember what my subject entailed, all I knew was that it was an assignment, and I needed to turn it in on time. When the teacher returned the papers to the class, she specifically gave me feedback. She said, "Alana, you know you could've been in honors English 4" …. I was not expecting that feedback considering the lack of effort that I put into the paper. I froze, I was in shock to hear those words because I did not expect that feedback from her. After getting over the shock, I welcomed her words. Throughout my educational life, I was picked on, felt judged, and verbally told that I was stupid. I felt that I was labeled, and I struggled with that feeling for years. Nevertheless, her statement to me on that day resonated with me and continues to be a reminder for me that there is something greater within me (which I knew all along).

Sunshine, I've had moments where no one was around to offer encouragement when I needed it most. A lot of the friends and family members who I was close with, down through the years we all just grew apart and ended up separating. So, for what seemed like the longest time ever, I had no one. No one to talk to, vent to, or confide in. It was just me and God. I began to just talk to Him and build my relationship day after day after day. In doing so, He taught me how to uplift my spirit. I learned that in my weakest moments, I had to be mindful and aware of what I think, listen to with my ears, and allow my eyes to see because they all were (and still are) contributors to how I handle things in life. I listened to music that ministered to my spirit, such as gospel and some old school. I took long walks, attended church as often as I could, and stayed close to God. And I began to cultivate my prayer life, which in return powered me up, all through the day.

Know that when you feel completely alone and need encouragement, beloved God is always available to you. Because encouragement starts with you, that is where God abides, in your mind and heart. You have the courage within you to believe in yourself when no one else does. Don't look for validation from others because God already has done so. It says it in His word. Allow your efforts to speak for you as God manifests those things into action. Like my mom tells me all the time, "The proof is in the pudding." And soon you'll find others being impacted by your life and encouraged, not realizing that it was God teaching you how to develop strength and courage within.

For years I had no friends, no one to encourage me, that was my age. During those long and hard years of my life, the only people I had were my circle which was my family (that I'm thankful to God for). But I had many moments where I longed to just have a relatable conversation with someone who didn't know me, who could be a real friend and encourager that I thought was needed during those times. I would constantly complain to my mom about feeling lonely and having no one to be there for me. I soon discovered that I needed to express these concerns to God. So, I started to draw closer to Him and He began to draw nearer to me.

Throughout this process, He gave me the reassurance I needed to help me overcome the feeling of loneliness. He filled that void.

What I learned was that when you have a strong desire for something and it doesn't happen at your desired time, you begin to idolize those very things, and this is against the will of God and is not how He wants us to think. God is more than able to give you the desired comfort and encouragement that you need, just open your heart to Him because He already knows what's in it. But He is waiting on you to lay it all before Him because He is not a forceful God. In Him, there is fullness of Joy. He is patiently waiting for you. So, allow Him to be that solid rock on which you stand because He is truly a friend like no other.

Chapter 8 Reflection

Encourage Yourself

Come unto me, all ye that labor and are heavy laden, and I will give you rest. Take my yoke upon you, and learn of me; for l am meek and lowly in heart: and ye shall find rest unto your souls. For my yoke is easy, and my burden is light. Mattew 11:28-30, KJV.

Self-Reflection:

Encouraging yourself starts within you, what actions have you taken?

_____
_____
_____
_____
_____
_____
_____
_____
_____
_____
_____
_____
_____
_____
_____
_____
_____

CHAPTER 9

Positive Patterns Equals Better Habits

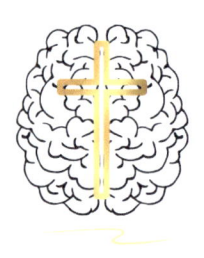

I understand sunshine, sometimes being positive can seem like it's no use. And sometimes you want to acknowledge your feelings for a while even if they are the total opposite. Because positivity is a choice. Right? And you may want to fester in that problem, issue, or whatever it may be. Know that that's fine too and is completely human. It's normal to feel as such. However, the main component of this is to not stay there. Because beloved, if you do, you'll begin to create problematic patterns unwarily, which in return becomes repetitive.

Now, I know that I've been talking about the mind a lot. But I can't say it enough, sunshine your mind controls everything about you. I decided to choose to change my mindset in ways that are conducive to my lifestyle, and that would permit better outcomes. Do I still have moments? Of course, I do! But they never define who I am. I feel them and acknowledge them for what they are, then immediately I relinquish them over to God. And I seek Him for guidance and then I leave them there. While doing so, I keep my faith anchored in God that He will prevail. And sure enough, He does, so let Him do the same for you.

One day I found myself communing with God like never before. I honestly never knew that love could feel like this. God is love! His love for us is really beyond what the mind can comprehend. One morning, I was at work sitting down at my desk, and I started to express my love to God. And within that moment, I felt His love overtake me in such a way that I was overwhelmed with His joy, peace, and happiness, and an expression of happy tears came about upon me, all because of His goodness. This happened because I was standing in gratitude to God for His presence in my life and for loving me so. Being grateful is the breeding ground for more, which brings an increase in every area of your life.

By adjusting my mindset, the flow of the day became more organized, despite whatever came my way, and my routine became more structured. Why? Because God is the center of my world and is at the very forefront of my life. He's my everything! I understand that I'm nothing without Him because I need Him every second of the day. On a personal note, this mindset alone caused me to produce better habits and it can surely do the same for you. Know that you control your thoughts and actions and not the world. So, make the necessary adjustments and you'll reap the benefits of it all in life.

Getting to know God is a personal journey. You will discover along the way who He is and have understanding and clarity in knowing that He is real. God desires to have a relationship with you because this is the catalyst as to how your faith operates through Christ within you. Faith without works is dead (it is an action word). Within your mind, begin to create better patterns that will in return permit better outcomes that are necessary for your lifestyle. Write them out and then put them to work. Soon you'll see how your life and way of living were inspired by just an act (or seed) of faith.

Chapter 9 Reflection

Positive Patterns Equals Better Habits

Finally, brethren, whatsoever things are true, whatsoever things are honest, whatsoever things are just, whatsoever things are pure, whatsoever things are lovely, whatsoever things are of good report; if there be any virtue, and if there be any praise, think on these things. Philippians 4:8, KJV.

Self-Reflection:

Hobbits are easy to form but sometimes not so easily broken. What will be the positive changes that will result in better habits for your life?

_____
_____
_____
_____
_____
_____
_____
_____
_____
_____
_____
_____
_____

CHAPTER 10

A New Lifestyle

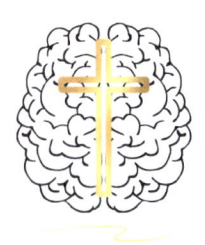

Reflecting on my childhood again, and even when my mother was pregnant with me (pastoring and preaching as I've been told), the church has always been a vital part of my life. I didn't have a choice being both of my parents were pastors. When I would go to church people would testify about the goodness of God, what He meant to them, and what He has done in their lives. I would be captivated by those who, in their previous life, had a different lifestyle, and had been through hell and back but one day their soul had a precious awakening that caused them to permanently change their life.

I believe from experience that change is always good, especially if it's for the betterment of yourself. But of course, it's by choice. I don't know about you sunshine, but when I have a made-up mind, I stand firm on what I'm choosing to do, and I go for it. Whether it's going for a nice walk or eating a piece of cake. I'm going to do it.

Our outcomes are a result of the choices we make in life. If we want better for our lives and our family; we must stop, take a step back, and do a self-evaluation. Discover what works and what doesn't work for your life. Determine what needs improvement, and how we can make life work better for us as individuals. Figuring out what strategies and methods will enhance your lifestyle is a self-motivator.

Sunshine, I don't have an answer as to how you select the right choice that is fitting for you or what will make your life easier. However, I will share past experiences with you about how I chose to implement a change that shifted my life, permanently. And it was all for my good.

From what I can remember, I've always had a relationship with God. Even as I grew up, I tried my best to always keep God in my life because my parents planted that seed. Just like that scripture in the bible that says, *Train up a child in the way he should go: And when he is old, he will not depart from it. Proverbs 22:6, KJV.* Even during my adolescent transition, I understood the importance of honoring God with my life because of the Christian values my parents instilled in me. While I understand that this is not everyone's story and it's perfectly fine if it isn't. Everybody's pathways and journeys are different and that is what makes you individually unique. The Bible says *I will praise thee; for I am fearfully and wonderfully made: Marvellous are thy works; And that my soul knoweth right well. Psalm 139:14, KJV.* He created and designed everyone in such a way that allows us all to have our own personalized identities in Him, that came from God. This is what sets you apart from others and is the difference in which He has made you to be.

During my time at Livingstone College in Salisbury North Carolina, every New Year's Eve, I made sure to make it my business to be present in the church, especially before the clock struck midnight. After giving God his time, I would leave the church to party with friends. I eventually came to myself and realized that God was not pleased with my double standards. It was then that I found myself at a crossroads and I needed to make a change. On November 8, 2020, I made up my mind that I wanted a completely new lifestyle for myself. Without all the distractions from no good relationships, sex, "and so-called friendships," my on-and-off struggle with marijuana, and black and mild's. And yes, I said it, black and mild (which is a tobacco product). I was engaging in all these things but deep down on the inside, I wanted to be free. My mother would tell me all the time to "stop, and put them down," but I wasn't quite ready yet (so I thought).

I remember this like it was yesterday. It was February 2015 at North Florida Cosmetology School in Tallahassee FL. My friend and I were at school, and we were sharing our thoughts about God's goodness and suddenly, God's presence filled the atmosphere, and we gave Him reverence. God's power pierces the very atmosphere we were in, right at school. And we both felt it, very strongly. God spoke through me to tell my friend, "You have been wanting to stop smoking these black and mild, and you've been feeling something in your throat." She answered, "Yes, I have, thank you, Lord." Next, I said, "You've been trying to stop, But God says He wants to deliver you today." She replied, "Thank you, Jesus!" Immediately after that moment, I felt led by the holy spirit to say a short prayer and afterward, we started praising God some more. Meanwhile, this entire time no one ever came back there to disturb the flow of the Holy Spirit, God just didn't allow it. Because deliverance was happening.

To this very day, it's been nearly ten years, and my friend has not smoked a black and mild sense. God completely removed the desire, taste, and residue that kept trying to linger from her life. Hallelujah! This is a testimony to the power of God who saves, heals, and delivers (and so much more). This was a new lifestyle change for her because she was a very heavy smoker.

Honestly, after that encounter with God, I still personally struggled with smoking black and mild myself and marijuana. I would try and stop. And then found myself doing it again. Then, something or someone would "trigger" me and I'd go right back to smoking them both again. I would often wonder why God would use me to help my friend get delivered when I desired to be, also. But it still hadn't happened yet. I was excited for her deliverance and still am. I concluded and realized that I needed to let go of it completely, stop trying to fight it in my own will, give it to God, leave it there, and put my faith to work. I was reminded of the scripture in the book of *Psalms 55:22, KJV* that says, *Cast thy burden upon the LORD, and he shall sustain thee: He shall never suffer the righteous to be moved.* So, I laid my burden down on the throne of Grace, upon the mercy seat, and proceeded to put my faith to work. And I have been delivered well over three years now. Every part of those bad habits is uprooted even the residue of them, and no lingering effects. They're all gone! Isn't God so good!!

Once you have a made-up mind to implement change, it will surely happen. It may not happen immediately or when you want it to but sure enough, I'm a firm believer that when it's your time, it will be right on time. But you must be determined enough to keep striving for the goal in view. And before you even notice, you'll find yourself changing.

Don't allow your past life, mistakes, and setbacks to deter you from the constant evolution of advancement. Because it is very possible. I know what It feels like to have setback after setback. Not knowing which direction to go while trying to figure out what is my God-given purpose? All this stuff is enough to completely stress you out, and bring about confusion, and negative thoughts that you haven't gotten peace about, within.

Beloved, God is saying let go and relinquish it over to me. In the book of *Philippians 4:7, KJV* says, *And the peace of God, which passeth all understanding, shall keep your hearts and minds through Christ Jesus.* You see, God wants us to put our burdens on Him and watch Him do the heavy lifting, and not ourselves. If it or that very thing is not working in your life, it may just mean trying something different. Because the right type of change will eventually permit improvement in that area and throughout your life in all areas as long as you live. Oftentimes, God's divine intervention will allow the necessary change/breakthrough that's needed at that appointed time and season within your life. But you must seek Him with your whole heart first. The Bible says so in the book *of Matthew 6:33, KJV says, But seek ye first the kingdom of God, and his righteousness; and all these things shall be added to you.* This is a promise from the supreme authority promise keeper.

A new lifestyle is just waiting to happen, just for you. If you truly desire it and realize that the right type of change is needed within your life, it shall come to pass. The first step is reconditioning your mindset, which will enable you to produce a new thought process, that in return empowers you to enforce the necessary changes that are conducive to your life and how it should be lived. Life is meant to be lived beautifully. Because it has so much to offer but you must have the proper guidance so that you can become and be your best self continuously, as you go from one level to another. It's about growth, advancement, and how you can learn to impact yourself, those around you, and abroad. God is the compass that leads you along the way and having faith in Him is the key that motivates you to keep striving for more.

There are things about yourself that you haven't even begun to discover. God is the revealer of all things. In the book of *Daniel 2:47, KJV* says it here, *The king answered unto*

Daniel, and said, Of a truth it is, that your God is a God of gods, and a Lord of kings, and a revealer of secrets, seeing thou couldest reveal this secret. He wants to be the wonder in your soul, meaning that He wants to reveal unto you the hidden things of Him about who you are that will help you to transform into the desired person that you are aspiring to be, according to His will for your life. If what you've been trying to do in your way hasn't been working, I recommend that you seek God for guidance, and He will direct your paths. Nothing is too great and mighty of a job that God can't handle. *For with God nothing shall be impossible. Luke 1:37, KJV.* Will you trust in Him for your change today? Know that He is the hope of your new lifestyle change.

Chapter 10 Reflection

A New Lifestyle

For with God nothing shall be impossible. Luke 1:37, KJV.

And the peace of God, which passeth all understanding, shall keep your hearts and minds through Christ Jesus. Philippians 4:7, KJV.

Self-Reflection:

A positive lifestyle change makes a better you, are you ready to begin?

_____
_____
_____
_____
_____
_____
_____
_____
_____
_____
_____
_____
_____
_____
_____
_____
_____

CHAPTER 11

The Knowing and Realization of You Are Never Alone

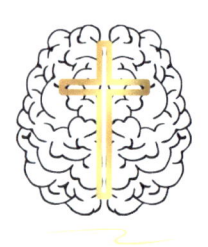

Let me ask you something, may I? Have you ever felt alone? And have you ever felt like you had no one to talk to or no one who understands? Be honest with yourself. I have. And I've been there as well.

Sometimes in life, you need someone to talk to who can relate to you. I recall a time when I had gotten to a place where my friendships and those who were connected to me were stripped away. I was alone. When it first happened, I'll admit it. I was lonely. It almost felt like God put me away like He was hiding me from the world. I was in isolation, unintentionally. It was an adjustment because I enjoyed having relationships with people. I would often see others fellowship when I would go out. And saw the laughter on their smiling faces, which indicated to me that they had a healthy and valuable relationship (so I thought). And I would say to myself, "It would be nice to have that." Even if it was just one person I could trust and talk to. But again, no one. I would have moments where my emotions would flair up because I felt like I needed a real and true friend, and there was no one to be found. So, I began to talk with God.

It was there when I started to verbalize myself to Him the most. I would have so much to say, most of the time. And honestly, I did most of the talking because of the lack of friendships. This process carried along for years. In my discovery, I got to a place where I realized that I needed to learn how to wait on God. So, I would posture myself to have quiet moments, without any music or any noise. Just complete silence. This was when I learned how to align myself with the spirit of God. It was during those many times that I learned how to be sensitive to his voice. So that I could become more familiar with His spirit when He would speak, and his presence would show up.

Next, I found myself fellowshipping with God. What this meant is that I had gotten to a level where He began to talk back to me. And I learned how to listen to the Holy Spirit. As I grew more in my fellowship with God, He taught me how to discern when He was speaking. So, this meant less talking and more listening. This was a challenge because I love to talk and be expressive, but He was conditioning me and teaching me discipline. God taught me who and where I put my dependency when the spirit of "loneliness" would try to creep in. He filled that void. And in doing so my relationship with God went to another level. I started to have intimacy with Christ, spiritually. My heart posture had gotten to a place where I began to delight myself in His love, His love for me, how He made me feel, and the love that I had and have for him even to this day. All of this kept me fueled up consistently. And from there I just grew intimately with Him, through His spirit. There is no manual as to how to explain this or how you can experience God on this level other than this. Welcome Him into your heart, space, and life. And allow Him to be God over you. Because He's not a forceful God. Be open and invite Him to do the work that's needed in your life and watch the manifestation of the miraculous take place, within your spirit and all around you.

Now, I can say that I have a few friendships today. Which I'm very grateful for. But first, looking back I had to go through those trying times to receive what I now have. Most of the time before we enter a new level or receive something new in our lives to advance us, we must be willing to learn how to wait. And I realize that it can be very uncomfortable. But the big question is this, how much are you willing to sacrifice, to get you to where you need to be right now in your life and beyond? Because after all, He sacrificed His life for you so that you may be saved, by simply believing in the power of His resurrection. In which is the Holy Spirit.

Maybe you are someone who needs to work on patience, practicing how to wait properly will strengthen you in that area and many others too. I'd like to share a scripture with you. Coming from the book of *Isaiah 40:31 KJV* it says, *but they that wait upon the LORD shall renew their strength; they shall mount up with wings as eagles; they shall run, and not be weary; and they shall walk, and not faint.* This scripture alone is proof that His spirit is there with us every step of the way as we go forward in His divine power.

Going through this process helped me to build up my personal relationship with God, on a level that I had never experienced. It was during this period of my life that I truly knew within my spirit, that God was a friend like no other. My confidence was up and when a person would ask me, "Who's your best friend?" I'd confidently say "God!" Some would say how or why?" He never turned His back on me, He loved me unconditionally, He brought value to every area of my life plus more, and still do. Because the love that I have for Him is completely indescribable. Words simply cannot express, the depth of my love for Christ, personally. He is the lifter of my soul. And ultimately, the love that He has for us all, there is none other greater. So, I encourage you to let God into your heart and there you will discover what real love truly feels like. Because you are never alone.

Think about this...Could it be that God has you alone, separated from others so that He can have your undivided attention because He knows that if you are occupied with people, stuff, and things, you won't hear nor see Him clearly in action? When God is trying to get your attention, He'll do whatever is necessary to let you see that He is the solution to any given issue you are faced with and wants to provide you with everything that you need so that you can be successful in life and spiritually. He wants you to be prosperous in all your ways. The Bible says it here in *3 John 1:2 Beloved I wish above all things that thou mayest prosper and be in health, even as thy soul prospereth.*

So, know that whenever you feel lonely His spirit is always accessible and available to you, no matter where you are or whatever may be happening to you or around you. God has an inexhaustible supply of His love and any and everything that you could ever need or want, and some and even more.

Chapter 11 Reflection

The Knowing and Realization of You Are Never Alone

Teaching them to observe all things whatsoever I have commanded you: and lo, I am with you always, even unto the end of the world. Mattew 28:20, KJV.

Self-Reflection:

You know where you've come from, and the purpose is great, now, will you pursue it?

_____
_____
_____
_____
_____
_____
_____
_____
_____
_____
_____
_____
_____
_____
_____
_____

CHAPTER 12

It's a New Day and a New You

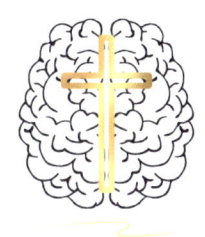

Have you ever found yourself getting caught up on the time you've wasted, or reflected on the mistakes you've made in your previous life? I know I have. And sometimes if you are not careful of being strong enough, those old spirits will try to inflict doubt, fear, negativity, and could potentially make you feel like you haven't changed at all. But know this, the devil is a liar in Jesus' name! Amen.

After overcoming those battles from the past, there are times when the enemy will try to use that old stuff to send discouragement and if not careful, you'll find yourself giving in to those negative thoughts. Finding ways that work for you such as walking to alleviate your stressors and situational events helps you maintain where you are so that you can continue progressing. I came up with a formula that

I like to speak over myself and my son, which is the word of God. *Psalm 51:10* KJV says, *Create in me a clean heart, O God; And renew a right spirit within me. And Let this mind be in you, which was also in Christ Jesus. Philippians 2:5, KJV.* There are times, if not cautiously minded, our spirits can get off track and it may not even be anything that you've done, per se. Sometimes life has a way of causing our moods to become altered by what we feel and what's happening around us. Your disposition could be completely positive, but your human nature may not be as aligned with your spirit as it normally is.

This is when you stop, step back, and acknowledge your feelings and emotions because they are relevant. Because it's your human nature to do so. And then you say to yourself, I realize that I feel this way now, but I cannot stay here. Then, this is when you begin to take control of the situation. When this happens to me because it still does occasionally, I acknowledge it and then motivate myself to have a positive outlook. And I begin to decree and declare the total opposite. Life! I speak life (according to God's word) to those things that try to disrupt my day and gain my control back.

We all have different routines as individuals in life. I have a routine that changes depending on where I'm at spiritually which may not work for you. However, I highly recommend that you commit your day, first thing in the morning unto God. This will start your new day on the right foot, despite whatever "pops up." And when it does, utilize the tools that generated that positivity when you woke up and refer to them. In some cases, you may even have to go as far as dismantling and canceling all attacks from that specific unclean spirit that would dare try to still the joy in your day. What you are doing is rebuking the spirit behind those things and or people who would try to inflict negativity and recentering your spirit back to where it needs to be. Because after all, just waking up to see another new day is a blessing. So, nothing and no one is worth the robbery of your joy and peace.

I learned how to live in gratitude, despite my circumstances. Because God daily loads us with His benefits, just like the bible says. Just think about it. He woke you up which is a blessing, you were able to dress yourself which is another blessing, brush your teeth, and your hair, walk, talk, hear, feed yourself, and beloved the list goes on. These are some of the many benefits from God to us all. It's more than enough to start your new day successfully. Listen sunshine, the new you may just require more so be willing to make the necessary adjustments when needed.

Your new day and new self can all be determined by what you're willing to see right in the mirror. You are resilient! Yes, you've been through many extreme things, but look how far you've come! You overcame it! So, don't you ever deny yourself the endless opportunities of having the privilege of seeing a new positive day. Because yesterday is gone. Press on in faith, trust God, and watch how things within you and all around you begin to look and feel different, in a good way. But you must be willing to embrace the change towards a better you. This should be enough to motivate you on your new path (give it a try because it works).

Find ways that are fitting for your lifestyle and turn your negative moments into creativity. Be creative in discovering ways to put joy back into your day. It could be something like turning on some worship music or listening to a person of influence to inspire and enlighten you and most importantly reading the gospel. Whatever alternative works for you, implement those new strategies and watch how your new daily pattern becomes more prosperous because of your decisions. Hold yourself accountable. And go on ahead and try it because it's a new you now and you owe it to yourself.

It is time to get excited about each new day and the new person that you are or may be striving towards. The thought of you transitioning from those old ways and mindsets into a new way of life, that is fulfilling is an amazing accomplishment, alone. Use the vehicle of joy to lead you into positive territories that can be building blocks of your faith and trust in the Lord. This mindset can give you the necessary fuel that's needed to give you motivation, determination, and commitment towards your goals in view, consistently. Use the power of God that is within you to command your day and live in His truths because He cares for you and wants you to live a life of prosperity, all your days.

Chapter 12 Reflection

It's a New Day and a New You

Create in me a clean heart, O God; And renew a right spirit within me. Psalm 51:10, KJV.

And Let this mind be in you, which was also in Christ Jesus. Philippians 2:5, KJV.

Therefore if any man be in Christ, he is a new creature: old things are passed away; behold, all things are become new. 2 Corinthians 5:17, KJV.

Behold, I will do a new thing; now it shall spring forth; shall ye not know it? I will even make a way in the wilderness, and rivers in the desert. Isaiah 43:19, KJV.

Brethren, I count not myself to have apprehended: but this one thing I do, forgetting those things which are behind, and reaching forth unto those things which are before, I press toward the mark for the prize of the high calling of God in Christ Jesus. Philippians 3:13-14, KJV.

Self-Reflection:

Praise God for a new day, leaving behind those things. Do you now see a new beginning in your life?

_____
_____
_____

CHAPTER 13

Life With Peace

I have found this to be so true. God will surely give you the peace that you need that is beyond your comprehension, but you must be willing to lay it all before Him and leave it there. Having peace in our lives is so necessary to us all. According to Bing, the definition of Peace is freedom from disturbances and promotes calmness. It is the vehicle that leads you on a path of wholesomeness that in return permits balance in every area of our lives. It is a tool that we all must learn how to use and be in as we strive daily towards who we are called to be as individuals.

I'm so thankful to God that I learned that absolutely nothing is worth the subtraction of my peace, joy, and happiness. Because I don't know about you beloved, but I've come too far to get to this place I'm at now in life to allow people, stuff, and things to be destructive in my space. No way, not here!

As you continue to journey through life with peace, you will begin to see life from a different perspective. It's very rewarding as well because you are in control as to what and how you allow things to affect you. When you are in constant prayer and in search of an answer from God, a confirmation sign is when you have the peace of God about what's in your spirit, whatever it may be. That is your answer.

Life is so much more than what society and the world have depicted it to be. It's meant to be demonstrated with love and balance. As you journey through life you will discover the unlimited diversities of harmonious rhythms, that all play a role in how you live and conduct yourself daily. The combination of this master peace, when played offers up a beautiful sound of peace ringing within your spirit and to others all around you. Life is more than superficial things, the ability to choose happiness is the prize. The Bible says that the joy of the Lord is our strength.

You are strengthened the most when you allow yourself to be in an uplifted state of mind. Something like smiling uplifts your spirits and those around you. No matter how you may feel, never stop smiling because it's a tool that keeps a sense of balance in your life and is also a weapon that can be used against the devil. Sometimes a simple smile can resolve or resurrect any dead situation. Know that the peace of God is the balancing influence that keeps you stable, durable, and ready to stand against anything that would try to come up against you. The weapons may form but as believers, we know that they will never prosper. So, may the peace of God be with you everywhere that you go continuously.

Chapter 13

Life With Peace

These things I have spoken unto you, that in me ye might have peace. In the world ye shall have tribulation: but be of good cheer; I have overcome the world. John 16:33, KJV.

Thou wilt keep him in perfect peace, whose mind is stayed on thee: because he trusteth in thee. Isaiah 26:3, KJV.

Peace I leave with you, my peace I give unto you: not as the world giveth, give I unto you. Let not your heart be troubled, neither let it be afraid. John 14:27, KJV.

Self-Reflection:

Life is beautiful, and the peace of God that comes with it is rewarding. Do you have peace today?

_____

_____

_____

_____

_____

_____

_____

CHAPTER 14

Wellness and Balance in The Mind

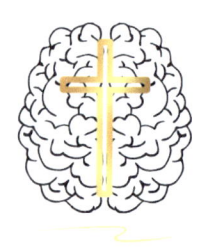

There is a renewal that's needed daily in each of our lives. *Romans 12:2 KJV says it here, "And be not conformed to this world: but be ye transformed by the renewing of your mind, that ye may prove what is good, and acceptable, and perfect, will of God."* Sunshine, you must get to a place where you purpose it in your mind that, if God be for you, who can be against me? Absolutely no one! Discernment is amazing to have because it can discern people, stuff, and things beyond what you see in the natural world that might just be a hindrance (there are different types of discernment). However, most importantly it also brings a spiritual awareness to rather if it is of God or not. If you should make that business decision or not and amongst many others.

The determining factor is your state of mind. How you select your choices will permit balance and how it is displayed within all areas of your life. You are a demonstration of what you think and feel within yourself. According to Bing's research Wellness is the act of practicing healthy habits daily that produce better physical and mental health outcomes. It's multifaceted, yet the main dimensions are spiritual, emotional, physical, and social wellness. These are all key components to a lifestyle of change, for the better and overall, and within your body. And it starts within your mind.

I'm a firm believer in the fact that you can't be as expressive about something if you haven't been through it yourself. How can you even begin to elaborate if you have not even experienced it? To be completely honest we all as individuals have a story and have at some point in our life gone through something that affected our thought process, either positively or negatively.

Testifying motivates you and gives you the empowerment that's needed to shift you at that moment to be powerful through God so that lives can be touched by you sharing your story. Let it be known to whoever needs to hear it. Don't be ashamed of it. Because it's a part of your testimony so that you can share and be a blessing to others, so that God may be glorified. Now that's advancing the kingdom of God down here on earth as He has commissioned us all to do! You may even be dealing with some of the most difficult things right now. But can I tell you that it will get better?

I know it sounds good and is so easy to say, but it's true. It all goes back to balance and your faith as you endure life. Knowing and understanding the word of God so that you can apply it to your life will surely help you implement the necessary balance that's needed. As I have mentioned before, dopamine in our minds is extremely powerful. If it begins to produce too much or too little our brains will become unbalanced. And our lives and lifestyles will reflect what's happening in our minds.

What works for me may not necessarily work for you, as we are all different and uniquely designed, individually. Take the time out and seek how you can bring calmness to your ragging sea. In other words, discover what helps you to have a sustainable and suitable quality of life, in all areas, especially when chaotic situations occur. Try new things and see If it works because you'll never know until you try it and see.

The next step would be learning how to maintain them all. This is what promotes structure in our lives, which in return gives balance and makes us all well within our minds. Whether you take medication or not. It will work just the same. God works through the medication because He made it to assist us (when needed) as we live from day to day. It doesn't mean that you don't believe that you aren't healed, but trusting God that He's going to move by his power through the medication to serve you according to how you need it for your body and lifestyle. Because truthfully you are already healed. *Isaiah 53:5 KJV* says it here, *But he was wounded for our transgressions, he was bruised for our iniquities:*

the chastisement of our peace was upon him; and with his stripes we are healed. Now, I understand how many would ask, but why do I have to take medication? Think about it… Could it be that God wants you to see that just maybe if I must go on medication and seek the necessary help, He's with me every step of the way? Would I put my pride aside and still trust God through it all? Despite what I'm facing or what type of change I need to make; He wants you to know that He is still fully able. But you must first remove self out of the way and allow God to be who He is in it and through it. Stop wrestling with it and trying to do it in your own will because I'm sure that you've reached many dead ends. Stop trying to figure it all out at once when He's already worked it out. Just be willing to surrender it all to Him and have faith that He will work it out for your good.

There are medications on the market that work, particularly for those who have mental health challenges. Honestly, most of us who struggle with it need medication so that we can have a better quality of life. But you must be willing to accept that you need help. God don't think that you don't trust Him. No, not at all. He's waiting to see if you will use the resources that are available to help you, to be well, which He has provided since the foundation of the earth. Think about it… Because He is the maker and creator of all things, this means that he made the resources from which the medication came about to help assist those who would need it. Everybody's story and outcomes are different. Some may only need it temporarily, some may need it on a short-term basis, and some may just need it for their entire life. And that's ok too. He wouldn't have made the provisions for the medication to be created if He didn't already know that many of us would need it. Why? Because He knew that it would be a great need for many all over the world. He does not forbid us from taking medication but wants us to use it so that we can be our best selves for Him, ourselves, our children, families, friends, and those surrounding us.

In the New Testament, Jesus Christ stated three times within the first three books of the new covenant that "those that are sick, needs a physician." The scriptures say it here as follows, *Matthew 9:11-13, And when the pharisees saw it, they said unto his disciples, why eateth your master with publicans and sinners? But when Jesus heard that, He said unto them, They that be whole need not a physician, but they that are sick. But go ye and learn what that meaneth, I will have mercy and not sacrifice: for I am not come to call the righteous, but sinners to repentance. Mark 2:17, KJV, And Luke 5:31-32 KJV.* You see, God is the Greatest Physician you'll ever need to help aid those who are sick. He didn't just come for the righteous but the sinners too. Jesus sat and ate with the sinners and healed many of them because only He had the power to do it. I believe He has given us His divine grace and mercy to utilize the appropriate medications to assist those in need of them because He is the Supreme Physician who has given us access to them. His preeminence power is working through the medication that overrules anything that would try to hinder the purpose of His glory being revealed while taking prescribed medication that brings about the transformation, healing, and balance that many of us need.

So, Use the positive methods and strategies that work just right for you. This is paired with learning about yourself and your body so that you can determine if it enhances your life or not. If you go to a doctor and don't care for that one, don't give up because of one bad turnout. Keep searching and be intentional about the help you are seeking. And please do pray for guidance because I can assure you that it works. Then, choose to be well despite what has happened or what you may be dealing with right now. Start by speaking it into the atmosphere, that it is well. I am well! We are well! As I have stated before, after it's all said and done, your mouth is a weapon. It can speak life or death. So use it properly as to how God intends for you to do so and get the necessary help that you need.

Chapter 14 Reflection

Wellness and Balance in The Mind

And be not conformed to this world: but be ye transformed by the renewing of your mind, that ye may prove what is good, and acceptable, and perfect, will of God. Romans 12:2, KJV.

But he was wounded for our transgressions, he was bruised for our iniquities: the chastisement of our peace was upon him; and with his stripes we are healed. Isaiah 53:5, KJV

And when the pharisees saw it, they said unto his disciples, why eateth your master with publicans and sinners? But when Jesus heard that, He said unto them, They that be whole need not a physician, but they that are sick. But go ye and learn what that meaneth, I will have mercy and not sacrifice: for I am not come to call the righteous, but sinners to repentance. Matthew 9:11-13, KJV.

Self-Reflection:

Transformation is an overall process. When the mind is made up you can pursue greater things. Are you willing to change your mindset?

_____
_____
_____
_____
_____

CHAPTER 15

Look How far You've Come

You are A Successor Because of Your Progression

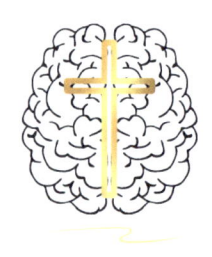

Wow! Beloved, have you ever sat down and reflected on your life? You have? Well listen, I'm sure you've seen growth in one area, maturity in another, and maybe a little weight loss and or gain (and that's ok too).

As you begin to think about how you arrived at this place you are currently, say to yourself, I made it through! I know that there were mistakes that happened and lessons that you learned. You may even have to make a big decision that changes the pathway you were once on. The loss of a loved one, a new marriage, a new addition to the family, the purchase of a new home, or car and much more may all be a part of your story. However, the reason why you and even I were able to overcome the afflictions in life, successfully and progressed onward is because of God. He alone has given us the power within the mind to discover and unlock the hidden jewels that are life-altering. That in return joins us to advancement within our lives.

I don't know about you. But when I think about my life, the good and the bad. I rejoice! And give God thanks. Again, as I have said previously. I truly thank Him for every no, rejection, heartbreak/ ache, setback after setback, disappointment, and honey the list goes on because they all helped to build my muscles so that I can endure this process called life. In my weakness bares strength. I would always find myself going through gracefully (unwarily during those times). There was an assurance that would always spring forth, just in the nick of time exactly right when I needed it. This was a reminder that my best is yet to come, as I like to say, and this is the same decree for you. Know that your praise is a weapon to the kingdom of darkness, and you should always give thanks unto God. A thankful heart brings an increase. And this is so true. I had to teach myself to always thank God, during the good, and the bad, when I felt like it and when I didn't. Sure enough, as I continued, I found myself advancing to another level in life, as I like to say, "striving in Grace."

Most of the time when we don't take the time out to pause and take a step back to see the positive changes we've already made in our lives and to see how far we've come, and how the new adjustment is working out for the greater good of ourselves and others around us. It can cause discouragement to creep in if not careful. Usually, a state of reflective thinking produces thankfulness, and it also flues you even more to keep pushing toward your destiny.

Know that it's ok to commend yourself, especially when you see a consistent rhythmic pattern of positive change that is adding more value to your life. This is to be acknowledged, even if it's only from you. Because you don't need anyone's validation or assurance but God. He is your validation, and He validates you. By doing so you will soon see how those places that had voids, are filled with Joy, laughter, peace happiness, and a sound mind. All, from God. Because you have discovered how to tap into the power of God, that lies within you, called faith.

Your faith can take you places that are beyond your expectations. But it's all according to what you believe even when you can't see it. This allows you to experience life, a new life at that on another level. Because your state of mind has been conditioned to operate differently. Your faith in God is what destroys any unbelief, despite whatever or whoever. This in return gives you access to dimensional manifestations one after another.

So, I encourage you beloved to do some reflecting. I can assure you that you'll be amazed at how far you've progressed, you'll find yourself going into praise and worship for God's goodness towards you, for what's getting ready to happen next, and for what is to come in your future. Be determined to uphold where you are right now in your life, steward it well, and be bolder and even more courageous enough to excel further beyond that place. Because you haven't seen your best days yet, greater is coming just for you!

Chapter 15 Reflection

Look How far You've Come

You are A Successor Because of Your Progression

Delight thyself also in the Lord: and he shall give thee the desires of thine heart. Psalm 37:4, KJV.

Self-Reflection:

Look how far you've come; your progression has been a success. What can you now tell others when you think about His goodness towards you?

_____
_____
_____
_____
_____
_____
_____
_____
_____
_____
_____
_____
_____
_____
_____
_____

CHAPTER 16

Maintenance and Up-Keep The Qualities of Life

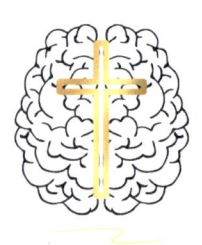

Sunshine! If no one has ever told you this before, it is with all pleasure that I say to you that you matter despite how others have made you feel, things, and situations. Know that your life matters. Your health matters. Your well-being matters, beloved! Why? First and foremost, you matter to God and therefore you should always matter to even yourself.

In life, as we strive daily to be better and to be the best that we can be, we find ourselves giving so much unwarily that we forget to pour it back into our cup. As the old saying goes, *"You can't give from an empty glass."* So, in most cases, we tend to neglect ourselves because of this. From there, it becomes a repeated cycle. We all have needs and things that help us to be more equipped to endure this process called life. Know that you and your life are a priority.

How you choose to upkeep yourself so that you can be the best you, no matter where you are currently, is a quality. This distinctive attribute should be a standard by which we as individuals should live by according to our lifestyles. Taking time out for yourself to just love you, to give your mind, body, and soul whatever type of maintenance it needs is vital. It is what allows a continuous flow of excellence to be produced from within you first and in return improvement over time within your life. Taking good care of yourself is important. Because you matter and your life holds great value. This mindset will surely enhance your overall quality of life, but you must be intentional and consistent when it comes to you alone.

This is one of the main reasons why God used me to write this book. To break the barriers against many of us called "stigma." These are tools that you can utilize as preventive measures. According to the *American Psychiatric Association*, *The National Alliance on Mental Illness* offers some suggestions about what we can do as individuals to help reduce the stigma of mental health challenges, such as talking openly about our issues (to trusted people), educating ourselves and others, being conscious of your language regarding the state of your one's condition, encourage equality, show compassion, and choosing to be empowered over shame are just a few strategies that you can implement as you press forward towards freedom from the stigmatized notion.

In 2018, after undergoing a test to pinpoint what medication would be most suitable for me. I learned about the different medications that are conducive to my DNA. That would assist me with the symptoms of bipolar and Insomnia. That moment in my life caused me to reflect instantly. It made all my sleep deprivation situations and manic episodes a bit clearer. Because now, when I don't understand something fully, whether it's this mental health challenge stuff or just life itself. I no longer fight with it or wear myself out trying to understand it all. Instead, I've learned to just rest in my assurance in God and trust that He never makes any mistakes. And then I find myself at peace and find solutions to solve my problems. Because this challenge does not define me. God does. It's just an avenue that He uses as I journey through life as a constant reminder to me, that I need Him, every day. God is so majestic, and He has a way of using things in our lives in whatever capacity He chooses to help us see that He wants to get the glory out of our lives and that He's able to do all things but fail. Look at my life. When I got to a place where I started to accept this challenge and not run from it. God in return taught me how to live not only with it but also be well and balanced in all areas of my life, even the more like never before. Because there is no sickness in God. You can be symptom-free. You are in control over it, and it does not have to have control over you.

Some would ask, Alana does it still affect you? And the answer is, yes. I do have my struggle moments, but I have learned from experience how to properly manage them even when they try to flare up. I had gotten to a place where I decided that I was no longer under its dictatorship and took back my power. I began to research natural supplements, teas, and the proper foods to eat according to my blood type. And became more knowledgeable in how I would posture my mindset before sleeping, such as quieting my mind (thoughts). I started exercising, praying more, and studying the word of God. Your upkeep may be completely different than mine and that's fine. Just always remember to prioritize yourself. I understand that we all have our individualized way as to how we maintain a certain level of quality in life, all according to what's needed and what we desire. Whether we are in a good and happy space or facing adversity. However, again being intentional about how we choose to care for ourselves properly increases longevity and permits an abundantly blessed life, overall.

Sunshine, keep allowing life to process you. And while doing so continue to trust God and never give up, no matter what. Allow your story to be the measuring tool as to how God will get the glory out of your life. And after He prevails and shows up strong, journey on and create another story, and so forth after that. Never stop creating and developing yourself. In doing so, this is how you discover the qualities in life that are uniquely tailored just for you. There is so much as to where God wants to take you and there is a lot that lies within you that you haven't even begun to tap into yet. So don't allow these issues and stuff to deter you from focusing on what matters most.

Family is very important to have because it's a necessity. Some of you may not have blood relatives to depend on, and that's ok too. Trust that God will send the right people at the right appointed time in your life. Knowing who to connect yourself to is extremely important. Because you need a solid support system, who you can depend on and refer to whenever there is a need in general. You need them and they need you too. It doesn't matter if they are blood relatives or not (in most cases the only connection you have with them is DNA). So many people don't know what it feels like to be loved. So, try something new. Take a leap of faith and open your heart! If God has blessed you with people who love you unconditionally, hang in there with them and continue building those relationships. And always remember to give God thanksgiving from your heart. Strive to do it daily and watch God reveal himself to you even greater. Be kind, patient and show love to yourself, and observe how your life increases and enhances in every area.

Know that you have everything you need lying right inside of you. Beloved, you can manifest your dreams and desires as to what God has in store for you, but you must believe. Your faith is the fuel that leads to the wonderful manifestations ahead and this is how you overcome warfare within the mind. So, keep trusting and do remember to always have faith, no matter how it may seem because your breakthrough is at hand. Knowing how to live out this life properly is vital, and understanding how to survive and thrive is even more important. These tools are what help you to overcome the many warfares in your mind Because God loves you with everlasting love. And you still have work to do, yes you!

Chapter 16 Reflection
Maintenance and Up-Keep
The Qualities of Life

Therefore, my beloved brethren, be ye stedfast, unmoveable, always abounding in the work of the Lord, forasmuch as ye know that your labour is not in vain in the Lord. 1Corinthians 15:58, KJV

Self-Reflection:

Maintain yourself as a good steward of what you have and always be anchored in your faith through Christ Jesus. Can you see the qualities beaming in your life?

_____
_____
_____
_____
_____
_____
_____
_____
_____
_____
_____
_____
_____
_____
_____

Alana's Proclamation

Everyone's healing doesn't happen in the same way. Most of the time, a lot of people are healed instantly, and they immediately recover from whatever sicknesses are in their bodies. Others may need to go through a healing process, which may require time. As for myself regarding the mental challenges I face, it's a bit different, not negating the fact that I'm already healed. However, my healing is from the operation of total dependency on God's grace and mercy towards me every day. Because without it I could never be completely anchored within my stance through Christ. I'm so thankful for His benefits that He daily loads me with.

I had goals of coming off the medication. But for now, I must take it. And yes, I do still consider myself a woman of God who has GREAT FAITH. Now I can see the manifestations of this every single day with clarity and a sound mind. It truly is a lot of courage and selflessness to lay aside my own opinions, feelings, pride, and emotions, and come to a place of acceptance for God's will for my life. Truthfully speaking, this was not and sometimes still isn't easy, but I've learned in this to just trust God through the process, Because He's building me up more and more, day by day so that I can withstand it all, regardless of what I'm unsure of. He is still moving by His power, making it all right and doable for me. And I know that He is with me always. So, receive your healing today because the price has already been paid in full just for you.

Acknowledgments

To my precious Jacob:

You have brought so much joy into my life and I truly thank God for you every day. Mommy loves you so much! I'm so thankful that at your tender age, you have a relationship with God and that *Psalms 91:1-2 KJV He that dwelleth in the secret place of the most High Shall abide under the shadow of the Almighty. I will say of the LORD, He is my refuge and my fortress: my God; in him will I trust.* It is your favorite scripture. I'm excited about your future baby because God has great things in store just for you. You are my angel!

To my parents:

Mama, thank you so much for teaching me about faith and demonstrating it so gracefully in all that you strive to do daily, in such a way that has transformed my life, and how you led me to this powerful scripture that has changed my life. I thank you for being there for me every time that I ever needed you, especially through all those torturous battles. And for really living out your life in this manner that in return taught me that, Now, *faith is the substance of things hoped for, the evidence of things not seen. Hebrews 11:1 KJV.*

Dady, thank you so kindly for modeling temperance (self-control), in all that you do, in every area of your life so beautifully and truly living out *Romans 12:19 KJV*. Daddy your spirit is just like *1 Peter 3:4, KJV which says, But let it be the hidden man of the heart, in that which is not corruptible, even the ornament of a meek and quiet spirit, which is in the sight of God of great price.* You naturally exemplify these characteristics well. I thank God as often as I can for specifically choosing the both of you to be my parents and I am forever grateful to Him.

To Jackie, my sister and mentor, thank you for modeling what it looks like to be content through all situations in life so eloquently despite whatever may be happening to you, within you, and around you. *Philippians 4:11 KJV says, Now that I speak in respect of want: for I have learned, in whatsoever state I am, therewith to be content.* I understand where your strength comes from and for this, I thank you, wholeheartedly. *Philippians 4:12-13 KJV.*

To Shelia my sister, I thank you for the true love that you have for your family that reflects God in you in a very special way. You demonstrate this scripture well and it says, *And the peace of God, which passeth all understanding, shall keep your hearts and minds through Christ Jesus" Philippians 4:7 KJV.* I truly appreciate you spreading the peace of God to everyone you encounter.

To my dear Aunt Verly, I truly thank you for teaching me in such a supernatural divine way that *No weapon formed against me shall prosper; Isaiah 54:17 KJV*, you have always said that they will form but will never prosper. You have imparted in my spirit how to tap into my faith in such a way that has produced the miraculous in my life, time after time, supernaturally. So, thank you for choosing to live your life as such because I am ever grateful unto God for you.

To Uncle Benny, I thank you for loving me and for being a representation of God's grace and mercy. *2 Corinthians 12:9 KJV, it says, And he said unto me, My Grace is sufficient for thee: for my strentgth is made perfect in weakness. Most gladly therefore will I rather glory in my infirmities, that the power of Christ may rest upon me.*

To DeAngelo, my brother. I thank God for you, for your heart, and for how it is a representation of God's love and for his people. So, *Let your light so shine before men, that they may see your good works, and glorify your Father which is heaven Mattew 5:16 KJV.*

To my late brother Kamali, thank you for teaching me that I don't have to prove anything to anyone and to just simply stay true to who I am.

Lastly, to all my family and friends who always show love towards me whenever we are together. I love you so much, indeed I do!

A Message from My Family to You

My name is Gloria Moore, the mother of Alana Starr Moore. As a child growing up, Alana has always been a healthy person. Nothing out of the ordinary that I had noticed signaling me concerning mental health during that time. It all became visible in her senior year in High School. I have been able to see and witness firsthand what mental health is like. It certainly was an eye-opener and many challenges for me and our family to see. The restlessness, the confusion of the mind, and the battle of fighting in the mind for survival were very difficult to bear witness to. Alana has always been a strong believer in her faith walk with God as a child in her earlier years. God has certainly gifted her in many ways. Alana has a very strong prayer life, and she knows the word of God.

When the mental health issues would surface and when she would go into distress, I would ask God, "Why my child?" Only to get an answer in return, "This will for her life will be for my Glory." I continued to persevere through it all with her through much prayer and fasting. Many family members did not understand mental health, so therefore it was overlooked with misunderstanding. A mother must always believe in her children, whether good or bad, even in mental health. I did it because loving her, caring for her, helping her, being there for her, and letting her know that she was not alone, brought me to the real knowledge of this challenge she has. I know that God is a deliverer, and he will set you free. It is my sincere prayer for you as an individual to continue to go forth with the blessings of God, inspiration, and encouragement as you start a new journey in life. From a mother's perspective, it gives me great pleasure to say, now that you are not afraid nor are you ashamed of mental health, the chains have been broken. Stay on the path of Hope, Peace, Steadfastness, and Joy threw Christ Jesus. And I quote, "What looked Impossible was made possible by God."

I have told my daughter many times and still to this very day, to never give up on your dreams. It is with all pleasure that I urge you to never do the same. Because it was the dreams that made me what I am and who I am today. From a young boy living in the country, in a house with no indoor plumbing. I always visualized myself having a loving family, in a nice home. During the earlier years of my pastoral ship, on my way to work, for a year, in passing I would see a construction site where houses were being built. I would claim by faith that one of those houses was going to be Gloria and my new home. As the months turned into days, before the development was fully completed, I dreamed of living in the sixth house on the right-hand side. And sure enough, just as God showed me, it happened exactly how I dreamed of it, and we are still living there today.

I want you to remember these scriptures and thoughts as a reminder to the seeds that are planted and all you have to do is nurture them and watch them sprout up. *Hebrews 13:8 KJV says, Jesus Christ is the same yesterday, and today, and forever. And Hebrews 10:35-37 KJV, says, Cast not away therefore your confidence, which hath great recompence of reward. For ye have need of patience, that, after ye have done the will of God, ye might receive the promise.*

The reason why I used these scriptures as examples is because I have watched Alana experience low and high moments with her mental challenges. Often, I would question, God why my daughter's life has come to this matter? Many times, in life God uses situations and circumstances for you to draw nearer to Him. I have seen Alana with her mental health challenge having no other way but to look to God and to depend on Him alone, instead of herself. And he brought her through every time, Glory to God! So, I encourage you to do the same, no matter how it may seem because there is always a way through Christ Jesus.

Alana Star Moore is a talented and gifted young woman. I'm extremely proud of her accomplishments. This book is fitting for anyone who is or has dealt with mental health issues. I remember when I had my first experience with my sister and her mental health episode. It was frightening and yet I had so much compassion and wanted to do whatever I could to help her. I remember putting her in the bed with me so that she could sleep, and I could keep an eye on her. When morning came, she made her way outside and talked to a neighbor, apologizing, and pouring out to her. I was determined that we would get help on that day. It was just me and her in this city. I drove to several locations to find help. In the first place, the doctor wanted to baker act her. I didn't know what it meant, but it could not have been good. He explained that it was involuntary admission to the facility. I questioned him, "How can this be involuntary when we are here, and she wants help? She is not a threat to herself, to others, or is dangerous?" We immediately left, because I was determined that she would not get caught in a system that wanted to confine her and possibly make her situation worse. We finally landed at a place where she could get the help that she needed, and I was allowed to visit and help my sister get better.

As I went through these experiences with my sister, I learned how to identify signs and symptoms of her episodes and we went through several of them together. During each episode, Alana maintained her faith in the Lord. She prayed and witnessed to the other patients (by the power of God miracles took place), she showed compassion, and she was loving and caring all while she was going through a mental health crisis. The nurses and doctors were amazed by her and her candidness. She sang songs for them and expressed her faith. She had an impact on them, she made them smile and filled the hospital ward with laughter. Oh, how vulnerable she was during these moments but so aware of who she was as a child of God.

Alana would write down her thoughts during these moments and we would read them after she was back to herself. Some of the things would cause us to laugh and some would be so profound because they were so deep even during those episodic times. This was a clear indication that God was using her mental health situation for His Glory to write this book to tell her story and to witness how God was with her. He gave her an understanding of what was happening to her and how she needed to begin taking care of herself. I remember how she rejected the medicines but when she acknowledged that it was to help her, she was able to work with her doctors to identify the best medicine to suit her. She turned to exercise, changing eating habits, and other holistic things that helped her maintain her health in her body, soul, and mind.

Alana is a prayer warrior and very determined to do whatever she sets her mind to do. When she started this book, she was going through some personal struggles. It was at this moment that she began to embrace and acknowledge that there's no shame in having a mental challenge. We have had many talks about mental health and how it can happen to the best of people, rich, poor, old, young, black, white, educated, uneducated, CEO, and grocery store cashiers. Many people, no matter their economic status, education, or race have learned how to live healthy and vibrant lives. I think that Alana has found her way to living her best life by sharing her story and speaking to other young people especially young black women and others abroad about mental health and overcoming the stigma and embarrassment of it. How to live healthy and live out your purpose. Alana understands that mental health is not a showstopper because you can be happy and feel normal. It's all about your manifest, your dreams in your life, and finding the power within to overcome them. I love you, Alana!

Your Sister,

Rev. Dr. Jacqueline Dowdy

My name is Rev. Verly Powell, Alana is my niece. I truly can say I am very proud and happy about Alana bringing this book forward. And to tell her story about what the Lord did in her life. God has worked miracle after miracle in Alana's life. I saw it first-hand. Miracles of healing, deliverance, and strongholds were broken by the power of God. She knew and learned how to wage warfare against the enemy well. Nobody could have done it but God working through her. I saw a great prayer life developed over the years and she took that same prayer life to reach out to help others with deliverance and healing. The spirit of the Lord increased on my lips as I witnessed it.

I can attest to this fact as to how deep her faith walk in God has been, and still is. Alana did not have a choice but to choose God because there was no other way. I have seen her at her lowest and weakest points in life. But God raised her up every time with victory. A lot of things formed but it did not trample over her. I know that this book will truly be a blessing to you and your life. Know that God wants to give you a marvelous testimony because if He did it for Alana, He can surely do it for you.

An Invitation to Salvation

I welcome those of you who are not saved, and maybe you were once before but are now in a backsliding state (meaning that you have somehow turned away from God). Know that God sent His son Jesus Christ to save the entire world from sin. So that means that He came for the sinners, and the unrighteous (saved or not). His gift to us all that He gave is salvation, which is deliverance from sins consequences, that includes death and eternal separation from God. But, having the opportunity of everlasting life within the Kingdom of God, forever more is your reward. To receive this gift of a lifetime is simple. Take your mustard-sized seed of faith and activate it.

Say this prayer of confession with me. Father, I believe in your son Jesus Christ, who died for my sins and who conquered death by the power of His resurrection. Father, forgive me for my sins. I repent, and I ask that you save me, Lord. I welcome you to be my God. I give unto you my life, as I start on this new path. Lord, I ask that you walk with me and guide me into all truths according to your word. Thank you for saving me. And I thank you for your unfailing love. In Jesus name, Amen.

The Response

I salute you in the name of our Lord and Savior Jesus Christ. And I welcome you into the body of Christ. Now that you are saved, I urge you to find a church that has a solid foundation of sound doctrine teaching the gospel (the word of God). It is very important to learn how to keep your faith anchored in Christ, how to live it out every day, how to have faith, and how to be in faith. They all work differently and together at the same time but are life changers as well. You will gain more insight as you begin to study the word of God and always remember to get understanding. Seek God and you shall find Him. Draw nearer to Him and watch Him draw closer to you. Know that your life will never be the same because you took that first step into freedom. You are officially free from captivity, so rejoice and give God praise and thanksgiving for the gift of eternal life you have received. May you prosper in all your ways, in every area of your life consistently.

Grace, Love, and Peace unto You,

Alana

References

King James Version of the Bible (KJV)

New International Version of the Bible (NIV

"Understanding Depression." *Psychiatry.org*, American Psychiatric Association, 2023, https://www.psychiatry.org/patients-families/depression.

Bing. (n.d.). *Search results for "define stigma"*. https://www.bing.com/search?q=define+stigma&qs=n&form=QBRE&sp=-1&ghc=1&lq=0&pq=define+stigma&sc=11-13&sk=&cvid=9C859835CE9F4864A8B620280205F598&ghsh=0&ghacc=0&ghpl=

Brues, A. (2023). *Circadian rhythm*. SleepDoctor.com. https://www.sleepdoctor.com/circadian-rhythm/

McDonald, M. (2018, September 19). *What is stigma?* **Medical News Today.** https://www.medicalnewstoday.com/articles/326649

Made in the USA
Columbia, SC
27 February 2025